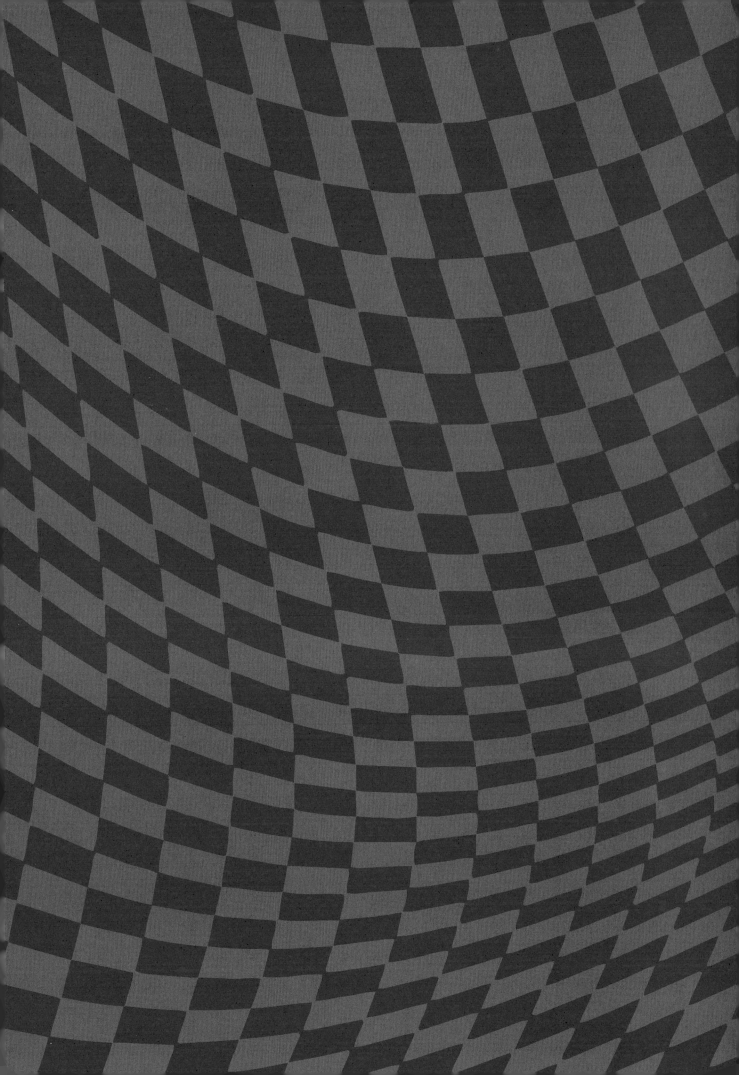

Thibaud Villanova

Gothic Recipes

PHOTOGRAPHER
Nicolas Lobbestaël

STYLING
Medhiya Kerairia

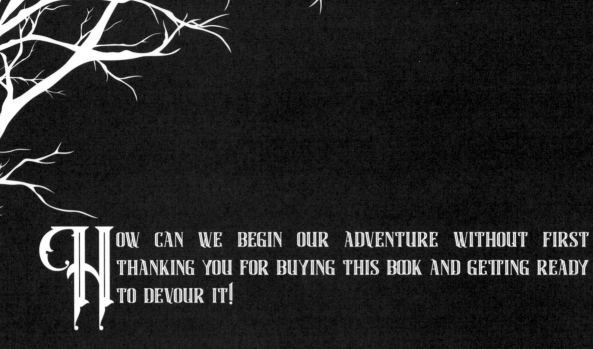

How can we begin our adventure without first thanking you for buying this book and getting ready to devour it!

If you're familiar with my work and my previous books, thank you for being so loyal; make yourself at home!

If, on the other hand, you're browsing the pages of *Gastronogeek* for the first time, I'd like to welcome you; you're about to embark on a ship that travels to the far reaches of imaginary cultures. For ten years now, my job has been to dissect pop culture works and their iconic dishes to teach you how to reproduce them at home. The idea is to allow you to prolong your immersion in cult references, to relive the great moments experienced by your favorite heroes or heroines, to sit down at the counter of a tavern in The Shire or at the table of a cantina on a planet in the Outer Rim, all without leaving your home.

And if you're not used to cooking, don't worry, my instructions are easy to understand. By browsing through the pages of this book and paying close attention, you'll learn the techniques and tricks that will help you feel a little more at ease in the kitchen every day.

All *Gastronogeek* books have this framework in common, but the book you are holding here is particularly dedicated to cult works steeped in the Gothic, the macabre, the fantastic and the magical. *Gothic Recipes* is a book that I've had in mind for a long time and that I'm delighted to present to you today.

I grew up with Tim Burton's films, marveling at the aesthetics of his characters, the darkness of his sets, the dark beauty of his monsters and the supernatural soul of his soundtracks. I've been listening to the themes of its composer, Danny Elfman, since I was 6 years old, and thanks to the *Gastronogeek* project and your support, I've had the privilege of being his private chef on two occasions when he came to Paris. Not to mention Guillermo del Toro's work and universe! Sometimes so gory, often dark and disturbing, always fascinating. I wanted to pay tribute to them by reproducing for you some of the dishes that have inhabited my imagination for the last thirty years: the biscuits of the creator of *Edward Scissorhands*, the Deetz cocktail in *Beetlejuice*, the pies at the Van Tassel banquet in *Sleepy Hollow*! But obviously, I wasn't going to stop at just two directors... That's why you'll also find recipes from *Supernatural*, *Evil Dead*, *The Addams Family*, *Buffy the Vampire Slayer*, *Luigi's Mansion*, *Crimson Peak*, *The Shape of Water*, *Hocus Pocus*, *Miss Peregrine's Home for Peculiar Children*, *Penny Dreadful*, *Frankenstein* and many more.

I hope this book will delight you and sometimes give you the chills, that it will make you want to cook for yourself, for your film evenings, and for your loved ones. Maybe you'll even do it while listening to Elfman on the night of a full moon. Who knows what might happen!

SETTING THE MOOD

MY PLAYLIST

I've always cooked or written while listening to music. Music transports me, making it easier to indulge my mental palate and my taste buds. So I thought I'd share with you part of the playlist I've created for myself and listened to over and over again while writing and designing this book.

▶ *Beetlejuice—Original Motion Picture Soundtrack*, "Main Titles", by Danny Elfman
This is one of the tracks that introduced me to the world of Danny Elfman, the brilliant composer behind some of the most fantastic and horrific soundtracks in Tim Burton's films.

▶ *Tim Burton's Corpse Bride—Original Motion*, "Victor's Piano Solo", by Danny Elfman
I've listened to this piano piece so many times in my life: 1'09 of simplicity, sweetness, and melancholy.

▶ *Sleepy Hollow—Music From the Motion Picture*, "Main Titles", by Danny Elfman
For me, it's one of the composer's most epic and sinister pieces; you can feel the darkness and macabre beauty of the different themes in the interwoven brass and choir.

▶ *Batman—Original Motion Picture Score*, "The Batman Theme", by Danny Elfman
There have been many versions of Gotham's Dark Knight since the 1960s. But there is only one work with such an iconic theme as Elfman's. I discovered Batman with Tim Burton's film and with Michael Keaton's face. This music is without doubt one of the craziest superhero themes ever.

▶ *Edward Scissorhands—Original Motion Picture Soundtrack*, "The Grand Finale", by Danny Elfman
The *Edward Scissorhands* theme, and this track in particular, is for me the most magical thing that has ever been composed. I listen to it when I want to dream, to cry, or to remember the film and its fabulous finale.

▶ *Tales from the Crypt—Original Music*, "Tales from the Crypt", by Danny Elfman
I associate this theme with my memories of horror when, as a child, I came across an episode of *Tales from the Crypt*. I link it to my reading of the novels *Goosebumps* and my first discoveries of children's horror literature.

▶ *Hocus Pocus*, "Main Title", by John Debney
A great theme song for three witches that I loved to hate!

▶ *The Addams Family—Motion Picture Soundtrack*, "Deck the Halls / Main Title", by Marc Shaiman
How do you combine the macabre, the gothic and the wildly romantic in a theme song? This theme perfectly illustrates the sinister, evil and terribly passionate side of Gomez and Morticia Addams.

▶ *Pan's Labyrinth*, "The Fairy and the Labyrinth", by Javier Navarrete
Pan's Labyrinth is the film with which I discovered Guillermo del Toro and his passion for monsters—whether human, like Captain Vidal, or from his fantastic and horrific bestiary. Javier Navarrete's soundtrack, and this track in particular, are masterpieces in my book.

▶ *Bram Stoker's Dracula—Original Motion Picture Soundtrack*, "Dracula—The Beginning", by Wojciech Kilar
I was far too young when I saw Francis Ford Coppola's *Dracula*; I should have been wary when I heard its theme, its construction... the tension and the evil that emanated from it. It's a perfect theme for your role-playing evenings or your gothic cooking evenings.

MY RECOMMENDATIONS

Don't know what to do while you're waiting for a stew to simmer or a pie to bake? You can't wait for Halloween season to begin and need to fill the time with pumpkin goodness and other activities? Then why not read a fantasy book or watch a horror film worthy of the name!

Here are my perfect picks to put you in the perfect supernatural mood!

 Sleepy Hollow, by Tim Burton
For me, it's the perfect film for Halloween; a cast that's just right, a plot that's as evil as it gets and a soundtrack that's sure to make your hair stand on end. I've been watching it every fall for over twenty years, and always with the same delight.

 Frankenstein; or, The Modern Prometheus, by Mary Shelley
How can you recommend Gothic literature without recommending Mary Shelley's *Frankenstein*? A chilling, dramatic, horrific and philosophical tale that blows the dust off the macabre genre.

 "The Fall of the House of Usher", by Edgar Allan Poe
In general, I recommend reading Edgar Allan Poe's short stories. *The Fall of the House of Usher* is a gem of horror that explores the themes of resurrection, the double and mental illness.

 The Addams Family, by Barry Sonnenfeld
The Addams Family was first created by Charles Addams as a comic strip, then adapted for American television in the 1960s. Nevertheless, whatever the versions and adaptations — successful or not — the most perfect Addams Family for me will always be that of Raul Julia and Angelica Huston, with Christina Ricci (a regular in films of the same genre) and Christopher Lloyd. This work is a gem of humor and darkness.

 Hellboy, by Mike Mignola
Hellboy is a comic book character created and drawn by Mike Mignola in 1994, and published by Dark Horse Comics. It's my reference comic. There's a *Hellboy* menu in my very first *Gastronogeek* book, and the drawings, scripts and adventures of the members of the BPRD have captivated me and stayed with me for over twenty years. Of course, you can watch Guillermo del Toro's adaptations, which are fantastic and respectable action films, but *Hellboy*, as a printed masterpiece, must be read and devoured!

Contents

In the mood 4

Utensils 10

Starters

Beetlejuice 15
Demonic prawn cocktail
King prawns, avocado and kiwi tartar, spicy cocktail sauce

The Witches 16
The soup's gone!
Pea, mint and goat's cheese soup

Demon Slayer 19
Tempura for Inosukee
Fried vegetables and king prawns

Doctor Stranger and the Multiverse of Madness 20
Poppa pizzas from the multiverse
Pizza balls with melted cheese and pepperoni

On the go

Casper 25
A ghostly breakfast
Fried chilli eggs, honey bacon, oatmeal and cinnamon pancakes

Dark Shadows 26
The Blue Whale sandwich
Tinned sardines, pepper mayonnaise and pickle sandwich

Supernatural 29
The Pizza of Death
Chicago-style pizza, provolone, marinara sauce

Main Dishes

Hellboy.. 33
Soup with Baba Yaga
Borscht and chicken casserole

Batman.. 34
Dinner with Vicki Vale
Escalope Milanese, tomato tagliatelle and peas

Sweeney Todd, the Demon Barber of Fleet Street.................................. 39
Mrs Lovett's Meat Pies
Beef cheek, pork and kidney pie with beer and vegetables

Dark Shadows...................................... 40
Willie's eternal roast
Gourmet pork roast with broccoli and potatoes

Bride of Frankenstein....................... 43
Feathered Chimera
Chicken and duck on the theme of "poultry corps-à-corps" by chef Alain Passard

Pan's Labyrinth................................... 44
The Captain's stew
Stewed oxtail, chorizo, baby vegetables (rabo de toro)

Dracula.. 48
Dinner on the first evening
Roast poultry and vegetables with paprika and cumin

The Lost Boys...................................... 51
The noodles of illusion
Fried noodles with vegetables and meat

Fullmetal Alchemist: Brotherhood........ 52
Gracia Hughes' quiche
Vegetable quiche

Luigi's Mansion.................................. 55
Mr Luggs' feast
Gigantic vegetable and cheese risotto

Castlevania.. 56
Trout a la Tepes
Baked trout with garlic and tomato

The Sandman...................................... 58
24H burger
Double meat, double egg, double bacon burger

Miss Peregrine's Home for Peculiar Children.......................... 63
Welcome turkey
Roast turkey and Brussels sprouts

Penny Dreadful................................... 64
A padded stew
Beef stew with beer

Desserts

It 69
Misfortune cookies
Biscuits with a message

Edward Scissorhands 70
A heart for Edward?
Lemon shortbread

Sleepy Hollow 73
Sweet pie from the Sleeping Valley
Apple, pumpkin and cinnamon pie

The Addams Family 74
Girl Scout cookies
Chocolate chip and macadamia nut biscuits

Wednesday 77
Masquerade fudges
Chocolate hazelnut and chocolate pistachio fondants

Charmed 78
Happy birthday Piper!
Chocolate cream cake

Carnival Row 82
Harken cake for tea
Vanilla and blueberry iced cake

Supernatural 85
Metatron's first waffles
Soft waffles, chocolate coulis, vanilla whipped cream and fresh strawberries

Buffy the Vampire Slayer 86
Jelly for Xander
Pomegranate and hibiscus jelly

Locke and Key 89
The rolls of remembrance
Cinnamon rolls

Crimson Peak 90
The Opera of Departure
Coffee and praline opera

The Shape of Water 95
Giles' favorite pie
Key lime pie with limoncello

Carrie 96
Margaret's apple pie
Apple pie with spices and cider

Drinks

The Magicians 101
Eliot's signature cocktail
Vodka, mint and bitters cocktail

Hocus Pocus 102
The Sanderson sisters' life potion
Apple, cucumber and kiwi detox drink

The Addams Family 105
Toxic lemonade
Lemon juice, tonic, elderflower and limoncello

Wednesday 106
The Yeti'tini of the ball
Lemon and curaçao syrup mocktail

Ash vs Evil Dead 109
Ash's pink fu**ck!
Vodka, strawberry and citrus cocktail

Evil Dead 110
Bloody party
Bloody Mary revisited

Tips

Sauces 114
Pastries and biscuits 116
Creams 117
Broths 118
Basic recipes 120
Culinary and gourmet lexicon 122
Conversions 128
Seasonal fruit and vegetables 129
The knives 130
Index of ingredients 132

The Utensils

Rectangle cookie cutter

Pressure cooker

Saucepan

Heart-shaped cookie cutter

Electric mixer

Kitchen blowtorch

Circular cookie cutter

Baking beads

Conical strainer

Kitchen string and trussing needle

Bowl

Cast iron casserole dish

Cocktail filter

Mixer/Blender

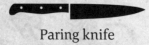
Paring knife

Whisk

Cocktail spoon

Waffle iron

Boston shaker

Mixing bowl

Fluted piping nozzle

Meat mincer

Beetlejuice
Demonic Prawn Cocktail

King prawns, avocado and kiwi tartar, spicy cocktail sauce

> There's nothing a demon enjoys more than haunting a house. Well, maybe driving a new family crazy is more fun. Who knows, the newcomers might be able to exorcise their meal? If not, they can call on that famous organic-exorcist, Beetlejuice... Beetlejuice... Beetle...

LEVEL ☠
Serves 4 people
Preparation: 20 min
Rest: 30 min

INGREDIENTS

20 large king prawns, already cooked

FOR THE COCKTAIL SAUCE
1 extra-fresh organic egg yolk
2 tbsp. mustard
⅔ tsp. (4 g) salt
⅘ cup (200 ml) vegetable oil
1 tbsp. ketchup or homemade tomato sauce (see tips p. 114)
1 tsp. tomato paste
1 tbsp. chilli purée
1 tbsp. whisky, cognac or brandy

FOR THE GREEN TARTARE
2 kiwis
½ cucumber
½ bunch fresh cilantro or parsley
2 ripe avocados
1 unwaxed lime (juice and zest)
1 tbsp. olive oil
⅓ tsp. (1 g) salt
⅓ tsp. (4 g) ground Espelette pepper

✦ Prepare a cocktail sauce with a bang: combine the egg yolk, mustard and salt in a mixing bowl and whisk or mix vigorously with a fork. While whisking, pour in the oil in a thin, steady stream. Mix until the mayonnaise forms. Add the ketchup, tomato paste, chilli puree and whisky. Check the seasoning by tasting and add salt if necessary. Your cocktail sauce is now ready. Keep it in the fridge until you're ready to serve, wrapping it in plastic wrap to prevent it from crusting.

✦ Move on to your avocado and kiwi tartare: peel the kiwis and dice the flesh. Peel the cucumber, remove its seeds, then dice it too. Finely chop the cilantro. Finally, peel the avocados and cut the flesh into larger cubes. Place the avocado cubes in a bowl and sprinkle with the lime juice. Coarsely mash the avocados with a fork, then stir in the kiwifruit and cucumber using a tablespoon. Add the chopped cilantro, olive oil and lime zest. Season with salt and Espelette pepper. Mix well and set aside for a few moments.

✦ Finally, shell the prawns, devein them, leaving the tails on, and proceed with the preparation.

DRESSING: Divide the fruit tartare between 4 tall glasses, serve with 5 prawns each and add 1 heaped tablespoon of spicy cocktail sauce.

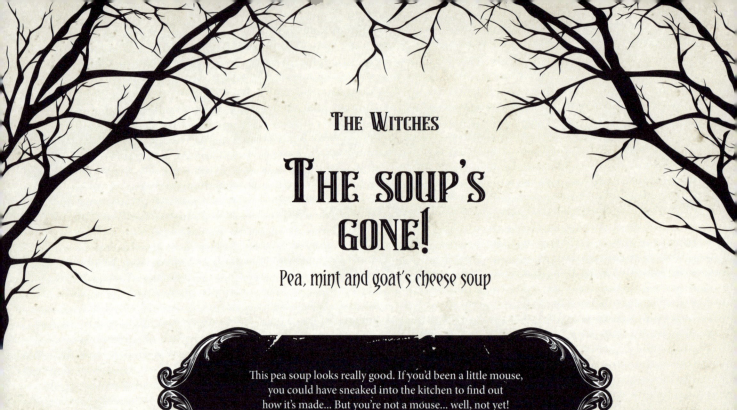

The Witches

The soup's gone!

Pea, mint and goat's cheese soup

This pea soup looks really good. If you'd been a little mouse, you could have sneaked into the kitchen to find out how it's made... But you're not a mouse... well, not yet!

LEVEL ☠
Serves 4 people
Preparation: 10 min
Cooking: 20 min

INGREDIENTS

2 ¼ cups (400 g) fresh peas
1 large potato
2 shallots
10 mint leaves
10 sprigs chives
2 tbsp. olive oil
4 cups (1 l) water or vegetable stock (see tips p. 118)
⅖ cup (100 ml) single cream (optional)
Ice cubes (for cold soup)
¼ cup (60 g) goat's cheese (Dorset, for example)
Salt, freshly ground pepper

EQUIPMENT
Hand blender

✦ Prepare the vegetables: rinse the fresh peas. Peel the potatoes and cut into small dice. Peel and chop the shallots. Also chop the mint and chives.

✦ Prepare a bowl of ice water. Bring a large volume of salted water to the boil and immerse the peas in it for 4 minutes, before draining them and plunging them into the ice water. After 30 seconds, drain and set aside.

✦ Pour 2 tbsp. olive oil into a saucepan and heat over a medium heat. Fry the shallots and potato pieces for 2 minutes before adding the water or stock. Cook for a further 10 minutes before adding the peas, half the mint, half the chives and the rest of the stock. Mix well and, using an immersion blender, blend until smooth. If the soup you obtain seems too thick, don't hesitate to thin it out with the remaining water or stock. Adjust the seasoning if necessary. For a smoother texture, you can also add cream.

DRESSING: Serve this soup hot or cold, blending it with ice cubes, for example. Garnish with the remaining mint and chives. Grate in some goat's cheese for an extra touch of indulgence and a nod to the Bournemouth region! Finally, finish off with a twist of the pepper mill to add a little heat!

Demon Slayer

Tempura for Inosuke

Fried vegetables and king prawns

The House with the Wisteria Family Crest is one of the best places for slayers to rest, regenerate and get ready to go demon-hunting again. According to the famous Inosuke, they serve an excellent vegetable tempura; the recipe is delicious and it's easy to digest!

LEVEL ☠
Serves 4 people
Preparation: 15 min
Cooking time: 2 min per batch

INGREDIENTS

12 raw king prawns
Salt
1 Japanese eggplant
1 zucchini
8 thin slices of lotus heart
8 green shiso leaves

FOR THE FRYING BATH
3 ⅛ cups (750 ml) organic rapeseed oil
3 ⅛ cups (750 ml) grape seed oil

FOR THE TEMPURA BATTER
¾ cup (100 g) organic flour
1 extra-fresh whole egg
1 cup (200 ml) water with ice cubes

TO SERVE
Tsuyu sauce (see tips p. 115)

✦ Prepare the prawns: peel them, leaving the tails on, devein them and salt them lightly on both sides.

✦ Wash and dry all the vegetables, including the lotus and shiso. Slice the eggplant diagonally and then into 3 mm thick strips. Cut the courgette into slices of the same thickness. Prepare a surface covered with kitchen paper or newspaper.

✦ Pour the 2 oils into a high-sided, thick-bottomed saucepan. Mix and heat to 170°C.

✦ While the oil is heating, prepare the tempura batter: sift the flour and set aside. Break the egg into a large mixing bowl and start whisking. Whilst whisking, add the flour in a dribble. Gradually stir in the ice-cold water. Your batter is ready when it has the texture of pancake batter.

✦ Once the oil has reached temperature, move on to cooking: dip the prepared vegetables, lotus, shiso and prawns in the tempura batter and then in the oil, for 1 minute 30 seconds to 2 minutes, proceeding by type of element, one after the other. Remove with tongs onto kitchen paper.

DRESSING: serve the tempura vegetables immediately to enjoy their crispiness. Serve with homemade tsuyu sauce.

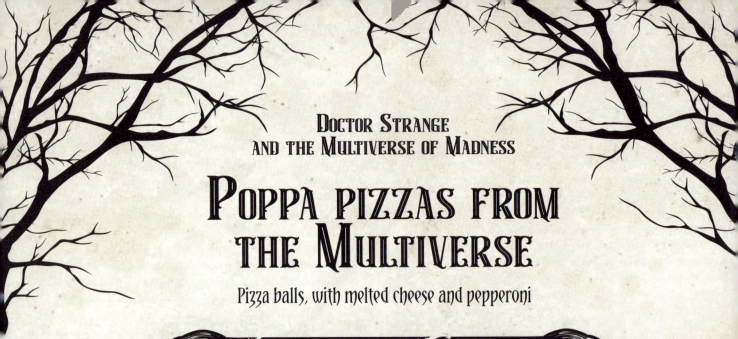

Doctor Strange and the Multiverse of Madness

Poppa pizzas from the Multiverse

Pizza balls, with melted cheese and pepperoni

Traveling between parallel worlds makes you hungry. Sometimes you have to hunt for your own food, sometimes it hunts you. Often, all you have to do is help yourself! The rest of the time, it can be useful to be friends with an Avenger who's a master of the mystic arts... Here's how to make the Poppa pizzas that America Chavez enjoys during yet another adventure with Doctor Strange!

LEVEL ☠ ☠
Serves 4 people
Preparation: 15 min
Cooking: 45 min

INGREDIENTS

½ cup (120 g) pepperoni or chorizo slices
⅔ cup (160 g) taleggio, reblochon or raclette cheese
1 ¼ cup (280 g) mozzarella
1 ⅔ cup (400 g) homemade pizza dough (see tips on p. 116)
Flour for the work surface

FOR THE TOMATO COULIS
½ cup (125 g) canned San Marzano tomatoes
⅓ tbsp. (2 g) salt
1 pinch dried thyme
1 pinch dried rosemary
1 pinch dried oregano

EQUIPMENT

8 muffin tins
Circular mini cookie cutter (optional)
Rolling pin

✦ Preheat the oven to 280°C (gas mark 9) or to the maximum setting. Place the muffin cases in the oven.

✦ Prepare the tomato coulis: place the tomatoes in a bowl. Wash your hands well or wear oven gloves and press the tomatoes between your fingers, crushing them thoroughly. Season with salt, dried thyme, rosemary, and oregano. Mix well and set aside.

✦ Cut mini slices of pepperoni from the large slices. To do this, use a small tube or a very small circular cookie cutter.

✦ Prepare the cheese: cut the taleggio into 20 g pieces. Cut the mozzarella into julienne strips. When cooking, it's best to squeeze it to remove as much whey as possible.

✦ Finally, move on to the pizza dough. Divide it into 8 portions of 50 g each. Flour the work surface before placing the dough pieces. Knead them for a few seconds, roll them out with a rolling pin and place a piece of taleggio in the centre. Close them over the cheese and seal well. Shape into balls and bake.

✦ Carefully take the muffin tins and place the cheese dough into the moulds. Drizzle with tomato coulis and top with julienned mozzarella and pepperoni, then bake for 10 to 15 minutes.

✦ All you have to do now is enjoy these Poppa pizzas and their melted cheese!

On the go

Casper

A Ghostly Breakfast

Fried chilli eggs, honey bacon, oatmeal, and cinnamon pancakes

Casper, the little ghost, may live with his three demonic uncles, but he's still a wonderful child, all too happy to welcome guests in his manor. This is just the kind of breakfast he could serve to Kathleen and her father James, his new flatmates!

LEVEL ☠
Serves 4 people
Preparation: 20 min
Cooking time: 15 to 20 min

INGREDIENTS

FOR THE PANCAKES
1 ½ cup (350 ml) oat milk
2 ½ tbsp. (35 g) butter
3 eggs
¾ tsp. (4 g) ground cinnamon
2 ½ tsp. (10 g) vanilla sugar
⅔ tsp. (5 g) salt
1 cup (130 g) flour
2 cups (180 g) rolled oats
1 ½ tbsp. (20 g) baking powder
Grapeseed or sunflower oil

FOR THE BACON
8 slices of bacon
2 tbsp. honey

FOR EGGS
⅓ cup (80 g) butter
12 eggs
12 pinches of salt
12 drops sriracha sauce
or Cholula® sauce

✦ Prepare the pancakes: pour the milk and butter into a saucepan. Cook over medium heat until the milk has become lukewarm and the butter has melted. Pour the eggs, cinnamon, sugar, and salt into a mixing bowl and whisk vigorously for 1 minute until the mixture is fluffy and smooth. Stir in the flour, oats, and baking powder. Add the milk and butter, mixing until the pancake mixture is smooth.

✦ Coat a frying pan with grapeseed or sunflower oil, heat over a medium heat and cook the pancakes until the batter is used up. Set aside.

✦ Place the bacon in a cold frying pan and heat over a medium heat. Cook for 4 minutes on each side and, after 6 minutes cooking time (after 2 minutes on the second side), drizzle the bacon slices with honey and cook for a further 2 minutes. Set the bacon aside on a small plate.

✦ Place the butter in a frying pan and heat over a medium heat. Once the butter has melted, break in the eggs. Sprinkle each egg with a pinch of salt. Put a drop of sriracha sauce in the centre of each egg. Cover the eggs and cook for a further 3 to 4 minutes.

DRESSING: serve 3 eggs, 2 slices of bacon and a few pancakes. Serve with a glass of freshly squeezed orange juice.

Dark Shadows

The Blue Whale Sandwich

Tinned sardines, pepper mayonnaise and pickle sandwich

The Collins canneries in Collinsport were the wealth of Barnabas's family for a long time before Angie Bouchard dismantled them. Here's a sandwich that could be served at the Blue Whale, Collinsport's seafarers' bar, where you'll have to go if you want to persuade Captain Clarney to fish for you…

LEVEL ☠
Serves 4 sandwiches
Preparation: 15 min
Cooking: 30 min

INGREDIENTS

1 red pepper
Salt
Olive oil
1 pinch of sugar
2 spring onions
4 tins of sardines
4 tbsp. homemade mayonnaise (see tips p. 114)
1 tbsp. maple syrup
1 tsp. bourbon
16 slices of sandwich bread
4 thick slices of lettuce or Batavia
Homemade red onion pickles (see tips p. 121)

✦ Preheat the oven to 220°C (gas mark 7). Prepare the vegetables: place the red pepper on a baking tray lined with baking parchment. Sprinkle with salt and a drizzle of olive oil. Bake in the oven for 30 minutes, then place the pepper on a sheet of aluminium foil. Set aside for 5 minutes, then remove the skin and stalk from the pepper and remove the seeds. Place the pepper in a blender with 1 tsp. olive oil, 1 pinch salt and the sugar. Blend vigorously for 30 seconds to obtain a red pepper coulis. Set aside.

✦ Rinse and pare the spring onions. Chop finely and place in a mixing bowl. Add the tinned sardines, mayonnaise, pepper coulis, maple syrup and bourbon. Mix well with a fork until you have a smooth filling.

DRESSING: For each sandwich, place a nice slice of salad between two slices of sliced bread and top with the sardine filling. Add a few red onion pickles for acidity. Enjoy this delicious sandwich before setting sail again!

SUPERNATURAL

The Pizza of Death

Chicago-style pizza, provolone, marinara sauce

> You really have to be Dean Winchester to save the city of Chicago from the clutches of Death. Luckily, this Horseman of the Apocalypse likes pizza.

LEVEL 💀💀
Serves 4 people
Preparation: 15 min
Cooking: 45 min
Rest: 1 h

INGREDIENTS

1 pizza dough (see tips p. 116)
⅔ cup (150 g) mozzarella cheese
¾ cup (200 g) provolone
½ cup (100 g) 'nduja or picante salami
½ cup (125 g) of canned San Marzano tomatoes
1 onion
1 stalk celery
1 clove garlic olive oil
⅔ tsp. (5 g) salt
1 tsp. (5 g) sugar
1 tsp. dried oregano
1 cup (100 g) grated Parmesan cheese

EQUIPMENT

Cast iron pizza pan or frying pan
Rolling pin

✦ Oil the pizza tin (or cast-iron pan) evenly. Place the pizza dough on top and roll out to a nice thickness using a rolling pin. Cover with plastic wrap and leave to rest in the fridge for 1 hour.

✦ Prepare the cheese: slice the mozzarella into julienne strips and place them in a drainer over a mixing bowl. The idea is to drain the mozzarella so that its whey doesn't soak into the dough. Cut the provolone into cubes or sticks. Strain and set aside.

✦ Remove the guts from the 'nduja and cut into small, meaty pieces (or slice the salami into small cubes). Set aside for later.

✦ Prepare the tomato sauce: pour the tomatoes into a large bowl and press them between your fingers. Set aside. Peel and chop the onion, then dice the celery. Peel, degerm and chop the garlic. Pour 2 tbsp. olive oil into a frying pan and heat over a medium heat. Fry the onion and celery in the oil for 5 minutes, stirring regularly. Add the garlic and cook for a further 3 minutes. Add the crushed tomatoes, salt, sugar and dried oregano. Mix well and reduce the sauce over a medium heat for 30 minutes, stirring regularly.

✦ Preheat the oven to 280°C (gas mark 9). Take the dish containing your pizza dough. Use it to line the tin as you would a pie, so that the pizza dough fits snugly into the tin. Chicago-style pizza is a pie with pizza dough. Place all the drained mozzarella and provolone on the dough. Add the 'nduja or salami. Cover with the reduced tomato sauce. Sprinkle generously with Parmesan. Finally, coat the pizza crust with olive oil and bake for 15 to 20 minutes.

✦ Remove the pizza from the oven and remove from the tin. Serve immediately.

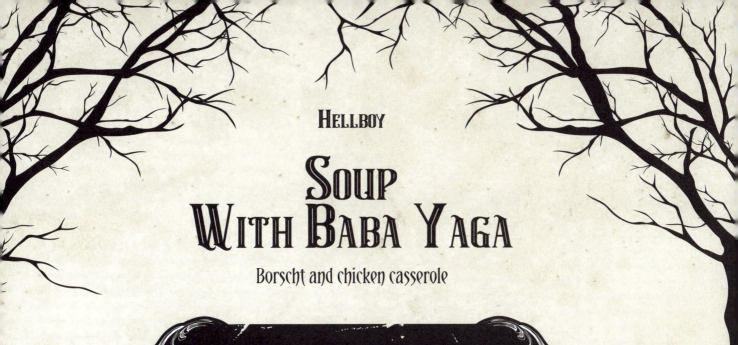

Hellboy

Soup With Baba Yaga

Borscht and chicken casserole

Nothing is more repulsive than the horrific face and emaciated, disarticulated body of old Baba Yaga. You have to sit down at the negotiating table but you're already wondering whether the soup she's serving you was made from the flesh of a child…

LEVEL ☠
Serves 4
Preparation: 15 min
Cooking time: 30 min in a pressure cooker or 1 h in a casserole dish

INGREDIENTS

4 large red beetroot
¼ green cabbage
2 carrots
1 onion
Salt
4 chicken thighs
2 tbsp. sunflower or grapeseed oil
3 tbsp. (40 ml) vodka
4 cups (1 l) chicken stock (see tips p. 119) or 4 cups (1 l) water + 1 tbsp. (15 g) coarse salt
1 tbsp. tomato paste
3 tbsp. (40 ml) wine vinegar
1 piece of marrow bone (ask your butcher)
1 bunch parsley

EQUIPMENT

Pressure cooker or cast iron casserole
Hand blender

✦ Prepare the vegetables: peel and chop the beetroot. Rinse the kale and chop coarsely. Peel and chop the carrots (they will end up in the blender). Peel and chop the onion.

✦ Salt the chicken thighs on both sides. Pour the oil into a pressure cooker or cast iron casserole dish. Heat over a high heat and once the oil is hot, add the chicken thighs. Grill the skin and sear all sides for 2 minutes 30 seconds, enough time to create the powerful juices that will give your borscht its body. Once the chicken is golden brown, drizzle with vodka and flambé. Add the beetroot, chopped cabbage, carrots and onion. Deglaze with 100 ml of the stock and use a wooden spoon to scrape up the juices from the bottom of the pressure cooker. Add the tomato paste. Reduce the heat to medium, stir well and then add the remaining stock (or water and salt) and vinegar. Add the marrow bone.

✦ If you are using a pressure cooker: close it tightly and fit the valve. Cook for 30 minutes from the first whispers. When cooking is complete, release the steam from the pressure cooker.

✦ If you are using a cast-iron casserole: cover and cook for 1 hour.

✦ Open and remove the chicken. Remove the skin and shred the chicken. You can reserve the bones for a more Baba Yaga style presentation. Set the meat aside. Use an immersion blender to blend the vegetables with the stock. Don't hesitate to add water or remaining stock if the mixture is too thick.

DRESSING: Finely chop the parsley. Divide the shredded poultry between 4 soup plates and top up with the stock. Garnish with the chopped parsley and serve piping hot!

33

BATMAN

Dinner with Vicki Vale

Escalope Milanese, tomato tagliatelle and peas

Bruce Wayne is a peculiar man, just as his mansion is huge and intimidating. The rooms are so big you'd almost have to shout for two people sitting at the same table to hear each other. So why not eat in the kitchen and meet Alfred, the fascinating butler, who will perhaps reveal the secrets of his rich protégé?

LEVEL ☠
Serves 2 people
Preparation: 20 min
Cooking: 45 min

INGREDIENTS
FOR THE TOMATO TAGLIATELLE
1 cup (200 g) fresh tagliatelle
3 large tomatoes
1 small red pepper
1 red chilli pepper
1 onion
2 garlic cloves
Olive oil
⅔ tsp. (5 g) salt
1 tsp. (2 g) pepper
1 ⅕ tsp. (3 g) ground Calabrian chilli pepper
1 tsp. tomato paste (optional)
¼ cup (40 g) fresh peas

✦ Preheat the oven to 200°C (gas mark 6). Prepare the sauce: remove the stalks from the tomatoes, pepper and chilli. Peel the onion and garlic. Place everything in a small ovenproof dish. Drizzle generously with olive oil and sprinkle with salt. Place in the oven for 25 minutes.

✦ Place the garlic and onion in the bowl of a blender. Peel and seed the pepper and chilli and place them in the blender. Blend vigorously for 1 minute to obtain a strong coulis. Set aside.

✦ Peel the tomatoes and place them in a bowl. Wash your hands and crush the tomatoes between your fingers. Pour the tomato coulis into a large frying pan and add the pepper coulis. Mix well and check the seasoning. Add pepper, Calabrian chilli and tomato paste if you feel the tomato flavor is not strong enough. Mix well and place over a very low heat.

✦ While the vegetables are cooking in the oven, bring a pan of salted water to the boil and prepare a container of ice water. Once the water is boiling, plunge the peas in for 2 minutes before placing them in the ice water for 20 seconds. Drain and add to the tomato sauce.

✦ Now prepare the Milanese escalopes. Beat the eggs and pour into a shallow dish. Pour the flour into another dish and the breadcrumbs into another. Stir the Parmesan into the breadcrumbs with the dried thyme. Set aside.

FOR THE MILANESE ESCALOPES
2 small veal escalopes
2 whole eggs
⅔ cup (80 g) flour
⅓ cup (40 g) fine breadcrumbs
¼ cup (30 g) grated Parmesan cheese
1 tsp. dried thyme
Salt, pepper
⅕ cups (50 ml) sunflower or grapeseed oil
1/4 cup (50 g) butter

TO SERVE
A few basil leaves
A few fresh thyme flowers
Grated Parmesan cheese

EQUIPMENT
Rolling pin
Blender

✦ Place the veal escalopes between 2 sheets of greaseproof paper and beat them a few times to flatten them. You can use a rolling pin, but don't take it out on the meat like Batman would on a thug—beating the meat too hard will break its fibres and make it difficult to chew.

✦ Salt and pepper the meat finely on both sides, then coat it with breadcrumbs; dip in flour, then beaten eggs, then breadcrumbs. If you want a crispier crust, dip the cutlets again into the beaten eggs and then through the breadcrumbs. Set aside.

✦ Pour 5 cl of grapeseed oil into a large, high-sided frying pan and heat over a medium heat. Once the oil is hot, place the breaded escalopes in the pan and brown them for 4 to 5 minutes on each side. Halfway through cooking, stir in the butter and baste the breaded cutlets well to give them a lovely golden colour. Remove the Milanese escalopes to kitchen paper and set aside for a few moments.

✦ Finish cooking the tagliatelle: bring a large volume of salted water to the boil and immerse the tagliatelle in it for 2 to 3 minutes. Remove the tagliatelle directly from the cooking water and dip into the sauce. Mix well and stir-fry the pasta in the sauce to activate the *mantecatura*, the bond between the sauce and the pasta.

DRESSING: serve one breaded escalope per plate and serve with tagliatelle. Decorate with a few basil leaves and fresh thyme flowers, then sprinkle with grated Parmesan.

SWEENEY TODD, THE DEMON BARBER OF FLEET STREET

Mrs Lovett's Meat Pies

Beef cheek, pork and kidney pie with beer and vegetables

Sometimes it doesn't take much to make a success of your meat pies: a devilishly lucky meeting, a bit of gumption, a... secret ingredient, and here you are, constantly cooking for hungry new customers!

LEVEL ☠
Serves 4 people
Preparation: 15 min
Cooking time: 1 h 45 in a pressure cooker or 2 h 35 in a casserole dish

INGREDIENTS
1.8 lbs (800 g) shortcrust pastry (see tips p. 116) or 4 discs of store-bought shortcrust pastry
Flour
Butter for the mold
2 egg yolks (for glazing)

FOR THE MEAT STUFFING
1.1 lbs (500 g) beef cheek
11 oz. (300 g) pork cheek
11 oz. (300 g) kidneys
Salt
1 carrot
4 shallots
1 garlic clove
2 tbsp. vegetable oil
⅔ cup (40 ml) whisky
1 sprig of fresh rosemary
1 sprig of fresh thyme
1 bay leaf
1 tbsp. flour
4 cups (1 l) beef stock
2 cups (500 ml) pale ale
6 juniper berries

EQUIPMENT
Ovenproof casserole or pressure cooker
4 small individual pie tins
Rolling pin
Food brush

✦ Prepare the stew to fill your delicious pies: cut the beef and pork cheeks into large chunks. Trim and coarsely chop the kidneys. Season all the meat with salt and set aside. Peel and finely dice the carrot and shallots. Peel and crush the garlic clove.

✦ If you are not using a pressure cooker, preheat the oven to 200°C (gas mark 6). Pour the vegetable oil into a casserole dish or pressure cooker and heat over a high heat. Add the meat and kidneys. Brown for 1 minute 30 seconds on all sides. Add the carrot, shallots and garlic. Season the vegetables with salt and brown for a further 1 minute, stirring well. Pour in the whisky and flambé. Add the rosemary, thyme and bay leaf and sprinkle with the flour. Mix well before adding the stock and beer. Check the seasoning and add the juniper berries.

✦ Cover the casserole and cook in the oven for 2 hours. If you have used a pressure cooker, close the casserole tightly and fit the valve. As soon as it begins to emit steam, turn down the heat to medium and continue cooking for 1 hour 10 minutes.

✦ Once the stew is ready, strain the mixture: separate the cooking juices from the rest. Coarsely chop the mixture and set aside. Pour the cooking juices back into a saucepan over medium heat. The idea is to reduce it gradually to obtain a sauce to accompany your pies.

✦ Preheat the oven (or lower the temperature) to 180°C (gas mark 4). Flour the work surface, divide the shortcrust pastry into 8 equal pieces and roll them out using a rolling pin. Butter 4 small pie tins and line each with a piece of pastry. Stuff them with the mince and then cover each with a piece of the remaining pastry. Seal the pastry tightly.

✦ Beat the egg yolks in a bowl and brush over the pies using a food-safe brush. Finally, cut vents in the centre of each pie to allow the steam to evaporate so that the pastry doesn't become soggy when cooked. Bake in the oven for 35 to 40 minutes.

DRESSING: serve a pie to each guest, accompany with reduced meat juices and enjoy piping hot!

Dark Shadows

Willie's Eternal Roast

Gourmet pork roast with broccoli and potatoes

Here's a gourmet version of the eternal roast that Willie cooks for the Collins family! There's no risk of it going dry, so everyone can enjoy it to the full!

LEVEL ☠
Serves 4 people
Preparation: 15 min
Cooking: 45 min

INGREDIENTS

1 kg roast pork loin
4 carrots
2 onions
3 cups (400 g) small potatoes
1 small broccoli
⅔ cup (150 g) lard or 4 tbsp. grapeseed oil
Sunflower or grapeseed oil
Fine salt, pepper
2 sprigs fresh rosemary
1 bouquet garni
3 cups (750 ml) vegetable stock or beef (see tips p. 118-119)
1 cup (250 ml) white wine

FOR THE ROAST STUFFING
5 cloves of garlic
3 shallots
4 tbsp. olive oil
Salt, pepper
1 tsp. dried thyme
1 unwaxed lemon (juice and zest)

EQUIPMENT
Oven-safe casserole dish
Small blender
Food string

✦ Prepare the aromatic stuffing for the roast: peel, and chop the garlic. Peel and chop the shallots. Pour the olive oil into a small frying pan and heat over a medium heat. Add the garlic and shallots to the oil. Season with salt and pepper and fry for 5 minutes, stirring regularly. Season with dried thyme and deglaze with the lemon juice. Mix well, then pour the mixture into the bowl of a small blender. Blend vigorously until you have an aromatic paste. Set aside.

✦ Now prepare the vegetables to accompany your roast: peel the carrots and slice them thickly. Peel and quarter the onions. Rinse and dry the beans. Rinse the broccoli and separate the tops from the heart. Set the tops aside and slice the heart. Your vegetables are ready, now move on to the meat.

✦ Preheat the oven to 210°C (gas mark 6-7). After washing your hands well, butterfly the meat; the idea is to use your chef's knife and cut the roast into a long piece 3 cm thick, which you will roll on itself, leaving the fat on the outside. Salt it lightly on both sides. Make incisions on the inside of the pork so that the aromatic stuffing can penetrate the meat. Coat the pork with the stuffing, then roll it up and tie it up. Coat with lard or oil and set aside.

✦ Pour 1 tbsp. sunflower or grapeseed oil into a casserole dish and heat over a high heat. Place the roast in the pan and sear on all sides for 1 minute 30 seconds before reducing the heat to medium and adding the vegetables. Season with salt and pepper. Add the rosemary and bouquet garni, then moisten with the stock and white wine. Stir and scrape up the cooking juices from the bottom of the casserole with a wooden spatula before placing in the oven.

✦ Leave to cook for 15 minutes. Baste the meat well with the cooking juices, then reduce the temperature to 180°C (gas mark 4), turn the meat over and cook for a further 20 to 25 minutes.

DRESSING: place the roast on a serving dish and serve with the vegetables. Pour the cooking juices into a sauce boat and serve immediately!

BRIDE OF FRANKENSTEIN

FEATHERED CHIMERA

Chicken and duck on the theme of "poultry corps-à-corps" by chef Alain Passard

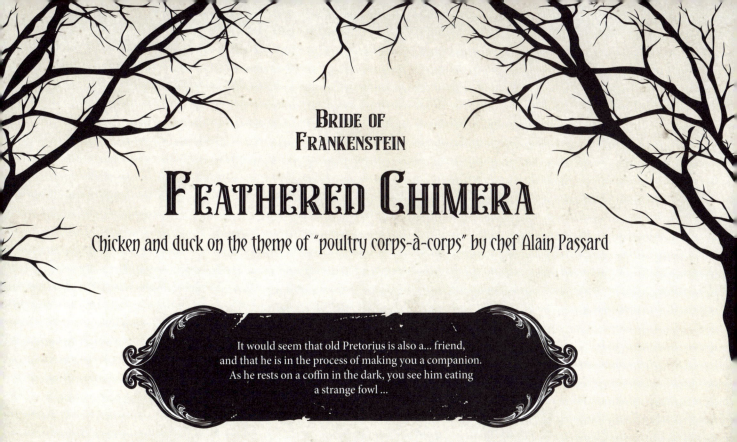

It would seem that old Pretorius is also a... friend, and that he is in the process of making you a companion. As he rests on a coffin in the dark, you see him eating a strange fowl...

LEVEL ☠ ☠
Serves 4 people
Preparation: 40 min
Cooking: 45 min
Rest: 40 min

INGREDIENTS

1 chicken weighing 1 kg, gutted and cut in 2 by your butcher and poulterer
1 duck weighing 1 kg, gutted and cut in half by your butcher and poulterer
8 small potatoes
4 carrots
2 cloves of garlic
8 brown mushrooms
1 sprig fresh rosemary
2 sprigs fresh thyme
16 cups (4 kg) grey Guérande salt

EQUIPMENT

Kitchen string and trussing needle

✦ Preheat the oven to 240°C (gas mark 9). Rinse the potatoes and carrots. Cut the potatoes into quarters, the carrots into wedges and crush the garlic under the blade of your knife. Soak a sheet of kitchen roll in water and gently clean the mushrooms. Cut into quarters. Set aside.

✦ Move on to preparing the chimera: get yourself some kitchen string and a trussing needle. The idea is to sew together, one against the other, the chicken half and the duck half. It sounds strange, but it's a cooking technique developed by the great French chef Alain Passard; you're going to experiment with the osmosis of flavors between the 2 meats. Tie the 2 birds together on the inside, spacing each stitch about 1 cm apart. Once the 2 carcasses are half sewn together, place the vegetables and herbs in the centre of the chicken half, and close the duck half over it. Continue binding, spacing each stitch as before. Your aim is to seal the birds perfectly.

✦ Pour some of the Guérande salt onto an ovenproof tray to make a salt well and place the chimera on top. Cover it with the rest of the salt, pressing the salt firmly against the chimera to form an even crust. Place in the oven for 45 minutes.

✦ Remove the baking tray from the oven and leave the poultry in a salt crust to rest for 40 minutes.

✦ Break the crust and release the bird.

DRESSING: Present the bird on a platter to your guests and cut into slices. Serve each person some chicken and duck. Serve with roasted vegetables and enjoy with a glass of red wine!

Pan's Labyrinth

The Captain's Stew

Stewed oxtail, chorizo, baby vegetables (rabo de toro)

Captain Vidal is a man of principle and rigour, a man who is not afraid of violence. No violence whatsoever. Not even the violence of discussing ration cards for the people while he and his guests, the notables, enjoy a banquet of traditional Spanish cuisine…

LEVEL ☠
Serves 4 people
Preparation: 15 min
Cooking time: 3 h 30

INGREDIENTS

800 g oxtail, tied
¼ cup (30 g) flour
4 carrots
2 mashed potatoes
2 onions
1 garlic clove
2 tbsp. grapeseed oil
3 cups (750 ml) red wine
2 cups (500 ml) beef stock (see tips p. 119)
1 cup (200 g) tinned crushed tomatoes
Salt, pepper

✦ This is my family recipe for *rabo de toro*. Salt the meat lightly on all sides. Dust with flour and set aside.

✦ Prepare the vegetables: peel and slice the carrots. Peel and finely dice the potatoes. Peel and chop the onions. Peel, degerm and crush the garlic.

✦ Pour 2 tbsp. grapeseed oil into a casserole dish and heat over a high heat. Once the oil is hot, grill the meat for 1 minute on all sides, before adding all the previously chopped vegetables. Deglaze with the red wine and use a wooden spatula to scrape up the cooking juices from the bottom of the pan. Add the beef stock and chopped tomatoes and check the seasoning: salt and pepper to taste. Cover and continue to simmer for 3 hours 30 minutes.

✦ Once cooked, carefully remove the meat from the casserole dish. Use an immersion blender to blend the cooking stock with the vegetables to make a thick, homogenous sauce. Check the seasoning and return the meat to the sauce until ready to serve.

✦ 30 minutes before the meat is due to finish cooking, prepare the chard and chorizo: remove the guts from the chorizo and dice. Remove the core from the chard and cut into pieces. Peel and chop the onion. Peel, degerm and chop the garlic.

FOR THE CHARD AND CHORIZO
⅓ cup (80 g) chorizo, strong or mild to taste
1 bunch of chard
1 onion
1 garlic clove
1 tbsp. olive oil

TO SERVE
½ cup (120 g) Manchego

EQUIPMENT
Hand blender

✦ Pour 1 tbsp. olive oil into a frying pan and heat over a medium heat. Add the chorizo and sauté for 2 minutes before adding the onion and garlic. Cook for a further 4 minutes, stirring regularly, then add the chard pieces. Season with salt, then add a ladleful of stock from the *rabo de toro*. Continue cooking for a further 10 to 15 minutes, until the chard has melted through. Set aside until ready to serve.

DRESSING: cut up the meat and place it in the sauce. Serve the dishes together in the centre of the table so that everyone can help themselves. Grate the Manchego over the meat and the chard before serving!

Dracula

Dinner on the First Evening

Roast poultry and vegetables with paprika and cumin

After a long journey from London, you arrive exhausted on the outskirts of Count Dracula's castle in Transylvania. An old man with white hair in a bun and a rich garnet coat welcomes you to his home. As he speaks and introduces himself to you, you are served roast fowl in sauce... This man seems to have a temper... of fire!

LEVEL ☠
Serves 4 people
Preparation: 30 min
Cooking: 40 min

INGREDIENTS

1 chicken weighting 1 kg, prepared and trimmed by your butcher
2 large beetroot
2 peppers
1 eggplant
5 garlic cloves, peeled
1 slice of farmhouse bread
½ bunch fresh parsley
4 tbsp. olive oil
1 tsp. ground paprika
1 tsp. ground cumin
1 tsp. ground cilantro
2 cups (500 ml) vegetable stock (see tips p. 118)
Salt

FOR THE MASHED POTATOES AND JERUSALEM ARTICHOKES
8 potatoes
4 Jerusalem artichokes
1 cup (250 g) coarse salt
1 ½ tsp. (8 g) fine salt
3 tbsp. olive oil
Pepper

TO SERVE
A few savory leaves

✦ Preheat the oven to 180°C (gas mark 4). Rinse the potatoes and Jerusalem artichokes. Place them in a saucepan and pour in 3 litres of water. Add the coarse salt and bring to the boil. Leave to cook for 15 minutes, until the potatoes and Jerusalem artichokes are cooked through. Drain and set aside.

✦ Peel the beetroot and cut into 6 pieces. Remove the stalks from the peppers, remove the seeds and cut into wide strips. Slice the eggplant. Crush 4 cloves of garlic under the blade of your knife. Set aside.

✦ Prepare your chicken: salt the inside finely. Rub the slice of bread with 1 clove of garlic. Place the bread, garlic clove and parsley in the chicken. Mix the olive oil in a bowl with the spices and 1 tsp. salt. Generously coat both the inside and outside of the chicken with the spice oil mixture, but do not use all of it.

✦ Place all the vegetables in an ovenproof dish. Place the spiced chicken on top. Moisten with the stock and drizzle the vegetables with the remaining spiced oil. Place in the oven for 40 minutes.

✦ While it's cooking, continue preparing the mashed root vegetables: peel the potatoes and Jerusalem artichokes. Place them in a large bowl and mash with a fork or using a potato masher. Add the fine salt and olive oil. Season to taste and set aside until ready to serve.

DRESSING: present the chicken to your guests on a platter. Divide the mashed potatoes and roasted vegetables between each plate, garnish with savory and use the cooking juices to finish seasoning!

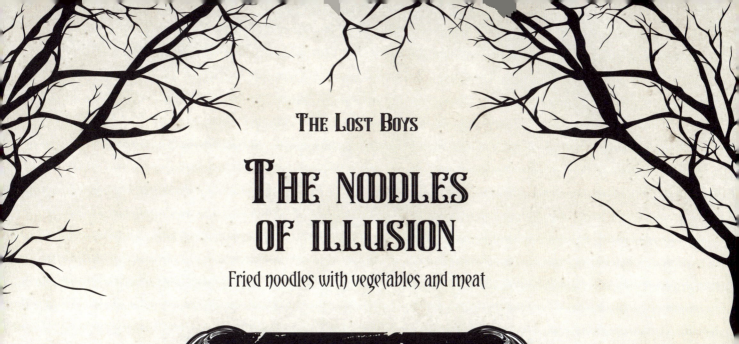

THE LOST BOYS

The Noodles of Illusion

Fried noodles with vegetables and meat

> After what David has done to you, you'll never be able to eat a bowl of white rice or order in a Chinese restaurant without thinking twice!

LEVEL ☠
Serves 4 people
Preparation: 15 min
Cooking: 15 min
Rest: 30 min

INGREDIENTS

11 oz. (300 g) pork tenderloin or beef flank steak
Salt, Sichuan pepper
1 tbsp. baking soda
4 cups (300 g) wheat noodles
1 new carrot
2 onions
½ cup (100 g) fresh green beans
½ cup (100 g) canned bamboo shoots
2 cloves of garlic
1 cm fresh ginger
2 tbsp. grapeseed oil

FOR SAUCE
5 tbsp. (70 ml) soy sauce
3 tbsp. (40 ml) Shaoxing wine
⅔ tsp. (2 g) five-spice blend

EQUIPMENT
Wok

✦ Prepare your meat: cut it into thin strips and place in a mixing bowl. Sprinkle with baking soda, salt and Sichuan pepper and mix thoroughly. Cover with plastic wrap and chill in the fridge for 30 minutes.

✦ Prepare the noodles: bring 3 litres of salted water to the boil and cook the noodles, stirring (to prevent sticking) for 7 to 8 minutes, until al dente. Drain and rinse quickly in cold water. Drain again and set aside.

✦ Prepare your vegetables: peel and finely julienne the carrot. Peel and finely chop the onions. Peel and halve the green beans. Drain the bamboo shoots and cut into julienne strips. Peel, degerm and chop the garlic. Peel and chop the ginger. Put to one side.

✦ Prepare the sauce: mix the soy sauce, Shaoxing wine and five-spice blend in a bowl.

✦ Move on to cooking: be careful, you'll need to stir constantly. Pour the oil into a wok and coat well. Heat over a high heat. Drain the meat and place in the boiling oil. Sauté for 1 minute before adding the vegetables and sauce. Stir-fry for 2 minutes before adding the noodles. Continue cooking for a further 5 minutes, stirring. Remove the wok from the heat and serve immediately!

FULLMETAL ALCHEMIST: BROTHERHOOD

Gracia Hughes' Quiche

Vegetable quiche

> You might say that your family situation is... complicated. You and your brother have been through so much already. It's so good to be welcomed as a friend and to be able to enjoy a moment of the Hughes family spirit over a good meal cooked by Gracia! And that quiche...!

LEVEL ☠
Serves 6 people
Preparation: 15 min
Cooking: 45 min

INGREDIENTS

7 oz. (200 g) homemade shortcrust pastry (see tips p. 116)
1 whole leek
1 onion
13 cups (400 g) fresh spinach
2 tbsp. olive oil
2 tbsp. (30 g) butter
Salt

FOR THE QUICHE MAKER
6 eggs
3 cups (750 ml) full cream
⅔ tsp (5 g) salt
⅔ tsp (2 g) cracked pepper
⅓ cup (80 g) Abondance cheese

EQUIPMENT
Tart or pie mold
Baking beans or dried beans

✦ Preheat your oven to 180°C (gas mark 4). Line a tart or pie tin with the shortcrust pastry. Prick the pastry base and fill it with baking beans (or dried beans) to prevent the pastry from swelling and shrinking during pre-baking. Place in the oven for 15 minutes. Remove the pastry from the oven, remove the baking weights and set aside.

✦ Prepare the vegetables: remove the rootlets from the leek and slice finely. Peel the onion and chop finely. Rinse the spinach and chop coarsely. Pour the olive oil and butter into a frying pan and heat over a medium heat. Place the vegetables in the pan, season with salt and sauté for 10 minutes, stirring regularly to prevent the vegetables from sticking. Set aside off the heat.

✦ Now prepare the quiche mixture: pour the eggs, full cream, salt and pepper into a mixing bowl. Whisk well until the mixture is smooth and creamy. Cut the Abondance cheese into small cubes and add them to the mixture with the cooked vegetables. Mix well and pour into the pre-baked shortcrust pastry base. Bake in the oven for 20 minutes.

DRESSING: serve this quiche cut into nice thick slices, accompanied by a green salad drizzled with vinaigrette!

LUIGI'S MANSION

Mr Lugg's feast

Gigantic vegetable and cheese risotto

How could Mario think you could win a mansion? It was a trap, and you're going to need all your willpower and your Ectoblast to get your brother out of this mess! You'll have to explore every room in this haunted house and confront the ghosts that await you... In fact, isn't that a ghostly emanation devouring a mountain of food right in front of you?

LEVEL 💀
Serves 4 people
Preparation: 20 min
Cooking: 40 min

INGREDIENTS

2 cups (200 g) chestnut mushrooms
2 zucchinis
⅔ cup (100 g) fresh peas
8 sundried tomatoes
1 onion
1 tbsp. grapeseed oil
Olive oil
4 cups (1 l) chicken or vegetable stock (see tips p. 118-119)
1 ½ cups (300 g) arborio rice
4 tbsp. (50 ml) white wine
Salt, pepper
1 cup (100 g) finely grated Parmesan cheese
¼ cup (30 g) finely grated Pecorino Romano cheese

✦ To preserve the beautiful colors of your vegetables and enjoy their authentic flavor, you'll need to be patient and organized, as you'll need to cook them in the right sequence.

✦ Prepare the vegetables: using a lightly dampened sheet of kitchen paper, gently clean the mushrooms. Cut into quarters and set aside. Rinse the zucchinis and dice them. Scoop out the peas. Finely julienne the sun-dried tomatoes. Peel the onion and chop finely.

✦ Pour the grapeseed oil into a frying pan and heat over a high heat. Place the mushroom quarters in the pan and sauté for 4 minutes without adding salt. The idea is to mark them and develop their earthy fragrance. Remove and set aside. In the same pan, pour 2 tbsp. olive oil and heat over a medium heat. Add the onions and zucchinis. Season with salt and fry for 8 minutes, stirring regularly.

✦ Meanwhile, prepare a bowl of ice water and bring a pan of water to the boil. Dip the peas in the water for 2 minutes before removing them and plunging them into the ice water for 10 seconds. Drain and set aside.

✦ Bring the stock to the boil in a saucepan. Pour 2 tbsp. olive oil into a large frying pan and heat over a medium heat. Pour in the rice and cook for 2 minutes, stirring well. The idea is to heat the grain without burning it. Pour in the white wine and allow to reduce before moistening the rice to the brim with the simmering stock. Let the rice absorb the stock and moisten again. When the rice has absorbed all the stock, taste it. Adjust the seasoning, adding a little salt if necessary. Moisten again and allow the rice to absorb the stock.

✦ Gently stir your risotto with a flexible spatula, while sprinkling the grated cheese over the risotto. If the rice is still too firm, add more water and stir until the stock is absorbed. Cooking takes between 15 and 18 minutes.

✦ Finally, add the peas, sun-dried tomatoes, zucchinis and onion to your risotto. It's ready to eat!

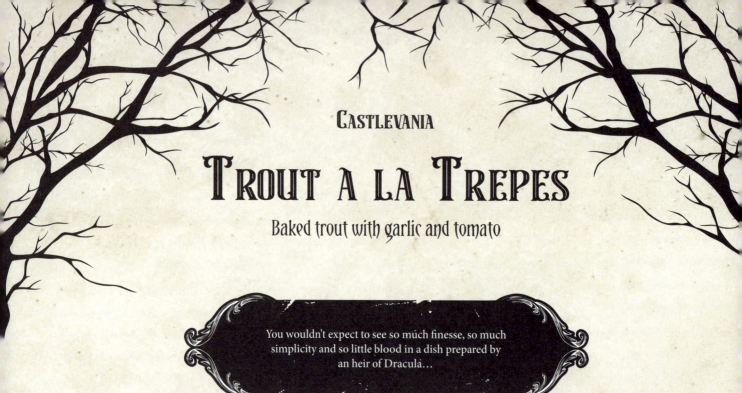

CASTLEVANIA

Trout a la Trepes

Baked trout with garlic and tomato

You wouldn't expect to see so much finesse, so much simplicity and so little blood in a dish prepared by an heir of Dracula…

LEVEL ☠
Serves 4 people
Preparation: 30 min
Cooking: 30 min

INGREDIENTS

2 trouts gutted and scaled by your fishmonger
4 cm fresh ginger
2 spring onions
2 heads of garlic
8 organic grape and cherry tomatoes
A few sprigs of fresh rosemary
Olive oil
Salt
A few sprigs of dried thyme
1 ¾ tsp. (5 g) ground chilli pepper

TO SERVE
1 small oak leaf salad
1 bunch of grapes

EQUIPMENT
Steam basket
Banana leaves (optional)
Food brush

✦ Preheat the oven to 180°C (gas mark 4). Prepare the vegetables: peel and slice the ginger lengthways. Rinse the spring onions, remove the rootlets and cut the onions lengthways. Cut the heads of garlic crosswise at the top of each head. Cut the tomatoes in half crosswise.

✦ Place the garlic in an ovenproof dish with the rosemary. Drizzle with olive oil and bake for 30 minutes.

✦ To cook the fish, bring a large pan of water to the boil and place a steamer basket on top. Place banana leaves, salad leaves or a sheet of greaseproof paper inside the basket. Salt the fish lightly, inside and on both sides. Stuff each fish with a chopped spring onion and a piece of ginger. Place the fish in the steamer basket and cook for 15 minutes.

✦ Meanwhile, prepare the tomatoes: pour 2 tbsp. olive oil into a frying pan and heat over a medium heat. Salt the tomatoes finely and place them in the pan. Cook for 4 minutes on each side and sprinkle with the dried thyme. Remove from the heat and sprinkle with the chilli.

DRESSING: serve 1 trout for 2 people, i.e. 1 fillet per person. Serve with grilled tomatoes. Serve the candied garlic cloves with the fish, along with a little salad (washed and drained) and grapes. Paint the fish with the cooking juices using a brush. Enjoy piping hot!

The Sandman

24H Burger

Double meat, double egg, double bacon burger

You're sick and tired of eating your greens. You could kill for that burger that's just been served at the next table, it's dripping. Juicy. Decadent.

LEVEL ☠
Serves 4 people
Preparation: 10 min
Cooking: 15 min

INGREDIENTS

4 homemade burger buns (see tips p. 120)
2 Baby Gem lettuces
2 tbsp. grapeseed oil
8 organic eggs
16 slices smoked bacon
Ketchup
Salt

✦ Shape your meat patties: peel and finely chop the onion, then the garlic and finally the parsley (if you have one, you can use a small blender or herb chopper to puree the onion, garlic and parsley).

✦ Wash your hands before handling the meat. (If you want to grind your own beef, use a manual meat grinder to do so. Chop the meat and its fat, then run it through the grinder and place it in a bowl). Sprinkle with baking soda and salt. Add the onion, garlic and parsley purée. Add the chilli puree and red miso, then knead the meat to combine all the ingredients. Press the meat between your fingers to bring out the collagen; your patties will hold together even better when cooked. Once the meat is well seasoned, divide it into 8 equal pieces. Roll them between your hands and toss each patty from palm to palm for 10 seconds; this will expel the air and make them denser. Set aside.

✦ Preheat the oven to 200°C (gas mark 6) on the grill setting. Rinse and coarsely chop the Baby Gem lettuces.

✦ Pour 2 tbsp. grapeseed oil into a large frying pan and heat over a medium heat. Gently crack the eggs to cook them in the pan. Use a 10 cm diameter circular cookie cutter if you wish to control their shape. Add a little salt. Cover and cook for 2 minutes, until the egg white has coagulated perfectly. Set aside for serving.

FOR BURGERS
1 onion
1 garlic clove
½ bunch parsley
2 lbs (800 g) minced beef or
2 lbs (800 g) rib steak
½ tsp. baking soda
1 ⅔ tsp (10 g) salt
1 ½ tsp. chilli puree
1 tsp. red miso

OPTIONAL EQUIPMENT
Small blender
10 cm diameter cookie cutter
Manual meat mincer

✦ Place the bacon slices in the same frying pan and brown for 4 minutes, turning halfway through. Remove and set aside for serving.

✦ Place the patties in the pan over a high heat (use 2 pans if you want to be able to cook and serve everything at the same time). Grill the meat for 1 minute on each side to obtain a nice, fragrant crust. Leave on the heat for at least 1 minute or longer, depending on how you prefer it cooked. Set the meat aside until ready to serve.

✦ Meanwhile, cut the burger buns in half and place in the oven for 1 to 2 minutes.

DRESSING: Assemble each burger in the following order, from the bottom to the top: coat the bun with ketchup, then cover with a little lettuce. Place a grilled steak and 2 slices of bacon on top. Top with a fried egg. Then top with a second grilled steak, 2 slices of bacon and another fried egg. Top with the remaining bread and pierce the burger with a wooden skewer to hold it together!

TIP
You can accompany this burger with a plate of fresh chips!

Miss Peregrine's Home for Peculiar Children

Welcome Turkey

Roast turkey and Brussels sprouts

Living at Miss Peregrine's seems like a particularly strange and fantastic thing to do. It's really going to take some getting used to… the company of the children you'll be spending time with. Perhaps sharing the gigantic turkey on the dinner table will help you break the ice!

LEVEL
Serves 8 people
Preparation: 20 min
Cooking time: 3 h

INGREDIENTS

FOR THE TURKEY
4 slices of farmhouse bread
2 cloves of garlic, peeled
One 7lbs (3 kg) turkey, trimmed and trussed
1 broccoli, cut into chunks
12 small potatoes
⅓ cup (80 g) melted butter
7 tbsp. (100 ml) sunflower oil
1 tsp. cumin
2 tbsp. maple syrup
1 tsp. salt + a little salt for the inside of the turkey
1 tsp. smoked paprika

FOR THE GARNISH
4 carrots
16 Brussels sprouts
2 stalks celery
1 ½ cups (300 ml) chicken stock (see tips p. 119)

✦ Preheat the oven to 200°C (gas mark 6). Prepare the turkey: rub the garlic cloves into the farmhouse bread, then stuff the turkey with them. Place the broccoli and potatoes inside the bird. Season the inside of the turkey with a little salt. Mix the melted butter with the oil, cumin, maple syrup, salt and smoked paprika and brush over the turkey. Set aside.

✦ Prepare the vegetable garnish: peel and halve the carrots. Rinse and dry the Brussels sprouts. Cut the celery into diagonal sections.

✦ Place the turkey in an ovenproof dish. Arrange all the prepared vegetables around the turkey and moisten with the vegetable stock. Cover with a large sheet of aluminium foil.

✦ Bake for 3 hours, basting the bird regularly.

DRESSING: serve up nice pieces of turkey to your guests and serve with vegetables and gravy!

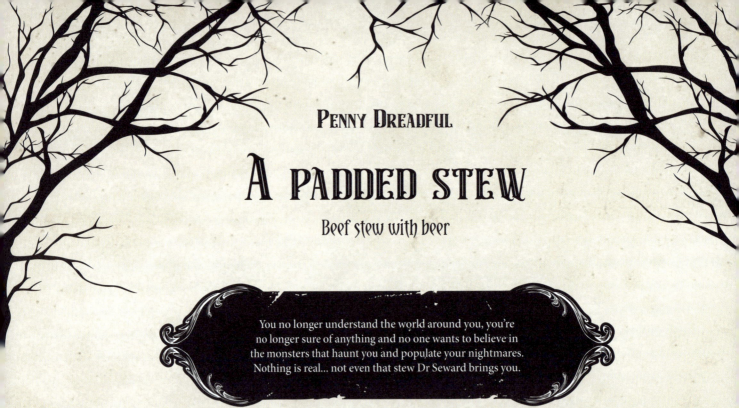

Penny Dreadful

A padded stew

Beef stew with beer

> You no longer understand the world around you, you're no longer sure of anything and no one wants to believe in the monsters that haunt you and populate your nightmares. Nothing is real... not even that stew Dr Seward brings you.

LEVEL ☠
Serves 4 people
Preparation: 15 min
Cooking time: 4 h

INGREDIENTS

2.2 lbs (1 kg) beef chuck
9 oz. (250g) smoked bacon
4 large carrots
8 potatoes
12 spring onions
½ head garlic
Salt
3 tbsp. grapeseed or sunflower oil
3 cups (750 ml) dark beer
4 cups (1 l) meat stock (see tips p. 119)
2 juniper berries
1 bouquet garni
1 cm fresh ginger Pepper

FOR THE SPINACH
5 cups (800 g) fresh spinach
⅓ cup (80 g) butter
Salt, freshly ground pepper

✦ Prepare the vegetables: peel and slice the carrots. Peel and halve the potatoes. Peel the spring onions. Crush the garlic in the palm of your hand.

✦ Prepare the meat: salt it lightly on all sides. Cut the bacon into large cubes.

✦ Pour the oil into a casserole dish and heat over high heat. Place the meat in the pan and marinate well on all sides for 2 minutes before reducing the heat to medium. Remove the meat from the pan and add the bacon. Brown for 1 minute 30 seconds, stirring well. Deglaze with the beer and scrape the bottom of the casserole with a wooden spatula to release the juices. Stir in the meat stock and return the meat to the pan with all the vegetables, berries, bouquet garni and fresh ginger. Mix well and cover. Leave to cook for 4 hours at a gentle boil.

✦ 30 minutes before the meat is due to finish cooking, prepare the buttered spinach: rinse and drain the spinach. Heat a large frying pan and melt 30 g of butter over a medium heat. Add the spinach, salt and the rest of the butter, cut into cubes. Cover and cook for 10 minutes ns over a medium heat. Remove the lid and stir well. Check that the spinach has melted and is well seasoned. Add a twist of the pepper mill and set aside until ready to serve.

DRESSING: serve the beef stew on a plate, with the spinach and accompanied by a fresh loaf of farmhouse bread to make the most of the sauce.

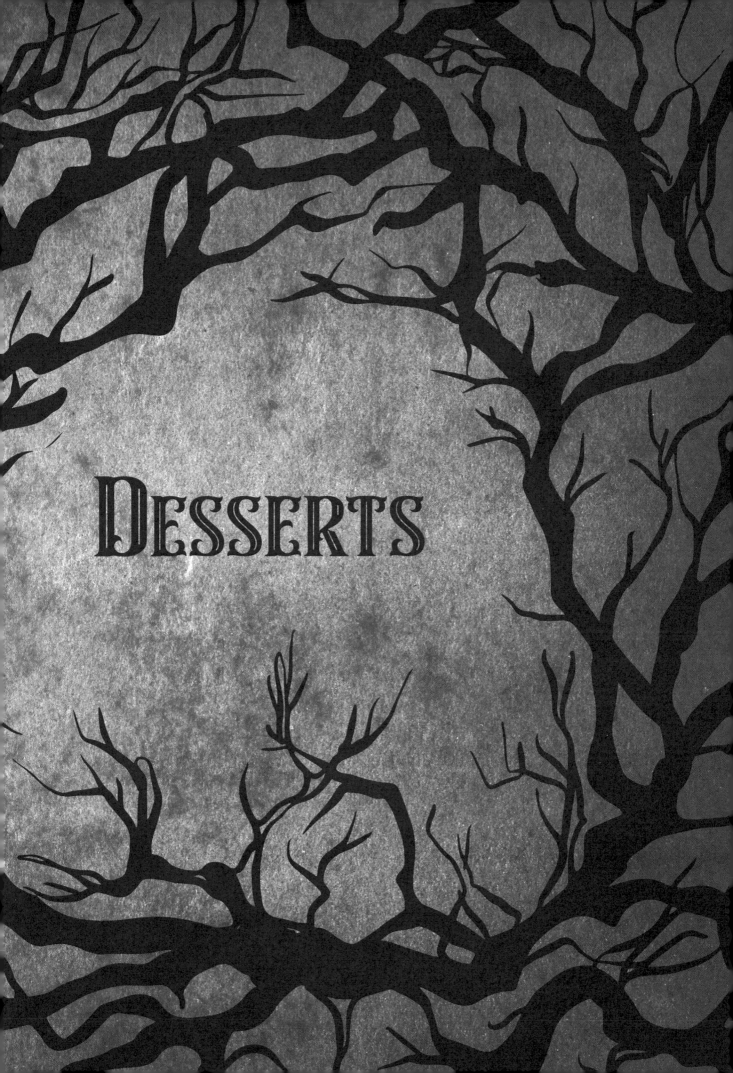

It
Misfortune cookies

Biscuits with a message

> It's been over twenty years since you last saw each other with The Losers Club, and here you are now, all round the table enjoying some fine Chinese cuisine. Only Mike seems preoccupied; he's talking about strange things happening in town again, warning signs. The same incidents that happened when you were children. Omens like fortune cookies releasing horrible creatures ready to attack you!

LEVEL ☠
Serves 4 people
Preparation: 15 min
Cooking: 7 min

INGREDIENTS

3 egg whites
5 tbsp. (60 g) sugar
6 tbsp. (80 g) melted butter
2 tbsp. almond extract
¾ cup (100 g) flour
3 tbsp. (20 g) ground almonds

EQUIPMENT

Silicone pastry cloth

✦ Preheat the oven to 180°C (gas mark 4). Pour the egg whites into a bowl. Add the sugar and whisk vigorously until the mixture is smooth and voluminous. While whisking, add the cooled melted butter and almond extract. Continue adding the flour and ground almonds.

✦ Pour the 10 cm diameter, 2 mm thick discs of the mixture onto silicone-coated baking trays. Bake for 7 minutes.

✦ Remove the baking trays from the oven and shape your biscuits while they are still warm: the edges should be slightly brown and the centre barely golden. Fold the discs in half. If you want to add a paper message to your biscuit, now is the time. Next, use a glass edge to hollow out the biscuit folded in half to give it its characteristic shape. Repeat the process with the rest of the biscuits.

✦ They're ready to eat!

Edward Scissorhands

A heart for Edward?

Lemon shortbread

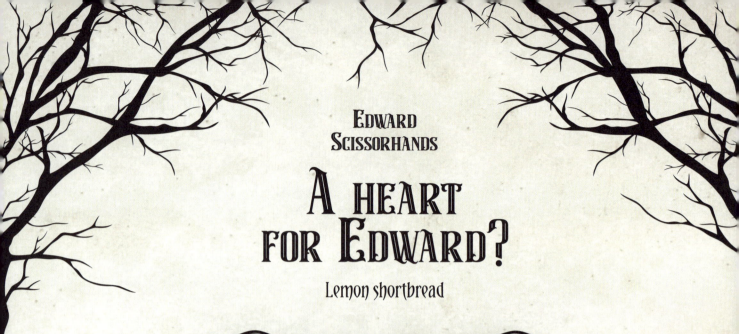

Do you know the story of a lonely old inventor who wanted to create a companion from a heart made of love and biscuits?

LEVEL ☠
Serves 4 people
Preparation: 10 min
Rest: 1 h
Cooking time: 10 to 12 min

INGREDIENTS

1 ½ cup (200 g) flour
½ cup (60 g) ground hazelnuts
7 tbsp. (80 g) sugar
3 tsp. (10 g) baking powder
1 pinch salt
½ cup (100 g) butter
2 tbsp. (40 g) homemade or store-bought lemon curd (see tips p. 117)
Flour for dusting
2 egg yolks (for glazing)

EQUIPMENT

Heart-shaped cookie cutter (optional)
Food brush

✦ Pour the flour, ground hazelnuts, sugar, baking powder and salt into a mixing bowl. Mix well. Cut the butter into cubes and rub into the dry ingredients. Stir in the lemon curd and shape the dough into a ball. Cover the dough with plastic wrap and refrigerate for 1 hour.

✦ Preheat your oven to 180°C (gas mark 4). Lightly flour the work surface and roll out the shortbread dough to a thickness of 3 to 4 mm. Use a heart-shaped cookie cutter or cut hearts out of the pastry with the tip of a paring knife.

✦ Place them on a baking tray lined with baking parchment. Brush the hearts with egg yolks to give them a golden hue after baking. To get the same heart-shaped cookies as in the movie, put them in the oven for 10 to 12 minutes.

✦ Remove the biscuits from the oven and leave to cool before serving.

Sleepy Hollow

Sweet Pie from the Sleeping Valley

Apple, pumpkin and cinnamon pie

> It's hard to believe that the village of Sleepy Hollow is the prey of a murderer when you arrive at the banquet given by the Van Tassel family. Watching the guests dance merrily and feast on delicious pies, it's hard to imagine them being terrified by a headless horseman…

LEVEL ☠
Serves 6 people
Preparation: 30 min
Cooking: 45 min

INGREDIENTS

2 homemade shortcrust pastry (see tips p. 116)
4 large apples (sweet or sour)
3 tbsp. (40 g) butter
4 tbsp. (50 g) brown sugar
2 ½ tsp. (5 g) ground cinnamon
1 ½ tsp. (3 g) ground nutmeg
2 tbsp. maple syrup
1 egg yolk (for glazing)
A few pinches brown sugar

FOR THE PUMPKIN AND HAZELNUT CREAM
⅔ cup (100 g) pumpkin
2 ½ tbsp. (35 g) butter, at room temperature
3 tbsp. (35 g) sugar
1 whole egg
4 tbsp. (35 g) ground hazelnuts

EQUIPMENT

Baking beans or dried beans
Food brush
Cake mold

✦ Preheat the oven to 200°C (gas mark 6). Cut the first pastry into strips. Place on a sheet of greaseproof paper and chill in the fridge. Line a thick cake tin with the second pastry. Using the tip of a fork, prick the base all the way round. Fill the pastry with baking beans or dried beans to prevent the pastry from puffing up or shrinking around the edges. Bake for 15 minutes, then remove the baking weights and leave to cool.

✦ Meanwhile, prepare the pumpkin and hazelnut cream: peel the pumpkin and cut into large cubes. Bring a large pan of water to the boil and immerse the pumpkin in it. In a large bowl, cream the butter (this involves mixing it until it takes on a creamy consistency). Add the sugar and then the whole egg. Mix until smooth, then add the ground hazelnuts.

✦ Once the pumpkin is cooked through, drain it, rinse it in cold water for a few seconds to cool it and press it into a purée. Fold the pumpkin purée into the hazelnut cream.

✦ Fill the pre-baked shortcrust pastry with the mixture. Bake for 10 more minutes, then set aside.

✦ Prepare the apples: peel them, core them and cut them into large quarters. Heat a frying pan over a medium heat and melt the butter, then place the apples in the pan and sprinkle with the brown sugar, cinnamon and nutmeg. Mix well and cook the apples for a further 5 minutes over a medium heat.

✦ Add the maple syrup and mix well. Continue cooking for 1 minute. Place the caramelized apples on top of the pumpkin and hazelnut cream. Cover with slices of shortcrust pastry from the fridge in a lattice pattern.

✦ Brush the egg yolk over the pastry strips. Sprinkle with brown sugar and bake for 20 minutes.

✦ Enjoy a slice of tart warm with a full-bodied cider!

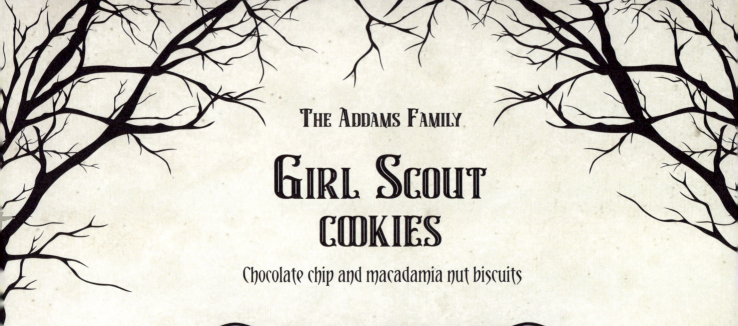

THE ADDAMS FAMILY

Girl Scout Cookies

Chocolate chip and macadamia nut biscuits

> Here's a box of cookies that those weirdos Wednesday and Pugsley aren't going to get! You were right not to swap it for their strange lemonade… "Are they made with real Girl Scouts?" What person in their right mind would ask such a question!?

LEVEL ☠
For 16 biscuits
Preparation: 10 min
Cooking: 12 min
Rest: 1 h

INGREDIENTS

⅔ cup (150 g) soft butter, at room temperature
7 tbsp. (80 g) sugar
1 tsp. maple syrup
1 tsp. vanilla extract
1 ½ cup (200 g) flour + a little for your hands
6 tbsp. (40 g) ground hazelnuts
1 pinch salt
1 handful macadamia nuts
3 oz. (80 g) milk chocolate chips
7 oz. (200 g) couverture milk chocolate

EQUIPMENT
Flexible spatula

✦ Prepare the biscuit mix: cut the butter into pieces and place in a bowl. Using a flexible spatula, cream the butter and, while doing so, add the sugar, maple syrup and vanilla extract. Mix until smooth.

✦ Sift the flour and ground hazelnuts and fold into the sweet butter mixture. Add the salt and mix again. Crush the macadamia nuts and milk chocolate and add to the mixture.

✦ Cover with plastic wrap and refrigerate for 30 minutes.

✦ Preheat your oven to 180°C (gas mark 4). Line a baking tray with greaseproof paper. Flour your hands and make the cookies: roll the cold dough into a long log 5 cm in diameter. Cut the roll into slices about 1.5 cm thick. Place the biscuits on the baking tray and bake for 10 to 12 minutes.

✦ Remove the biscuits from the oven and place on a wire rack to cool.

✦ Place in the fridge for 20 minutes.

✦ Meanwhile, melt the couverture chocolate in a bain-marie. While you're waiting for it to melt, place a wire rack over a small bowl, a mixing bowl or a casserole dish. Place the cold biscuits on the rack and pour the melted chocolate evenly over them. Leave to stand for 15 minutes, just long enough for the chocolate to harden, and you're ready with delicious chocolate-coated cookies!

✦ Enjoy them now or put them in a tin to enjoy later!

Wednesday

Masquerade Fudges

Chocolate hazelnut and chocolate pistachio fondants

To carry out your investigation at Nevermore, you'll need to blend in with the crowd and take part in group activities. And that means helping to sell chocolate treats to the tourists who've come to take part in Outreach Day!

LEVEL ☠
For 32 sweets
Preparation: 10 min
Cooking: 10 min
Rest: 1 h

INGREDIENTS

FOR THE CHOCOLATE-HAZELNUT FUDGE
16 oz. (450 g) milk chocolate
1 tbsp. hazelnut purée
1 ⅕ cups (300 ml) sweetened condensed milk
1 ½ oz. (40 g) hazelnuts

FOR THE CHOCOLATE-PISTACHIO FUDGE
11 oz. (300 g) white chocolate
1 tsp. pistachio purée
1 ⅕ cups (300 ml) sweetened condensed milk
2 drops of green food coloring
5 oz. (150 g) dark baking chocolate

EQUIPMENT
Cocktail sticks
Square mold

✦ Prepare the chocolate hazelnut fudges: chop the chocolate and place in a bowl. Add the hazelnut purée and sweetened condensed milk. Place the bowl in a bain-marie and melt everything together. Mix well to blend the ingredients together. Once the mixture is liquid and smooth, pour in the hazelnuts and mix again.

✦ Line a square baking tin with greaseproof paper and fill with the mixture. Smooth out the mixture and place in the fridge for at least 1 hour. Your fudge is ready!

✦ Remove the mold from the fridge and cut the fudge into small cubes. Stick them on a wooden skewer and serve!

✦ Prepare the chocolate-pistachio fudges: chop the white chocolate. Pour it into a mixing bowl with the pistachio purée, 100 ml of sweetened condensed milk and the food coloring. Place the bowl in a bain-marie and melt everything together. Mix well to blend the ingredients together.

✦ Line a square baking tin with greaseproof paper and fill with the mixture. Smooth out the mixture and place in the fridge for 10 minutes.

✦ Chop the dark chocolate and place in a bowl. Pour 200 ml of sweetened condensed milk over the chocolate and place the bowl in a bain-marie. Melt everything together. Mix well to blend the ingredients together. Once the mixture is liquid and smooth, pour it over the previous mixture.

✦ Smooth the mixture well and refrigerate for 1 hour.

✦ Remove the mold from the fridge and cut the fudge into small cubes. Stick them on cocktail sticks and serve!

Charmed

Happy Birthday Piper!

Chocolate cream cake

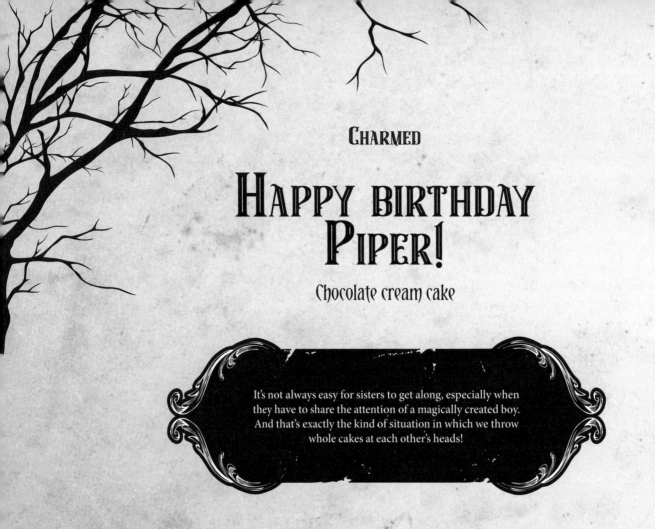

It's not always easy for sisters to get along, especially when they have to share the attention of a magically created boy. And that's exactly the kind of situation in which we throw whole cakes at each other's heads!

LEVEL
Serves 6 people
Preparation: 40 min
Rest: 30 min
Cooking: 35 min

INGREDIENTS

FOR THE CAKE
10 fresh strawberries
5 tsp. (25 g) butter + a little for the tin
4 whole eggs
1 pinch of salt
½ cup (120 g) sugar
7 tbsp. (100 g) flour
5 tsp. (25 g) bitter cocoa powder

FOR THE STRAWBERRY SYRUP
⅔ cup (150 ml) water
2 tbsp. (30 g) sugar
1 ½ tbsp. (20 ml) strawberry liqueur

✦ Preheat the oven to 180°C (gas mark 4). To whip well, the cream must be whipped with very cold utensils. Place a bowl and the whipping attachment in the fridge. Hull and quarter the strawberries.

✦ Melt the butter in a saucepan over a low heat and remove from the heat. Break the eggs and separate the yolks from the whites. Pour the whites into a large bowl and sprinkle with salt. Whisk the egg whites until stiff and set aside.

✦ In another bowl, pour in the yolks and add the sugar. Using a whisk, whip the yolks vigorously until you obtain a frothy, creamy mixture with plenty of volume. Set aside. Carefully mix the flour and bitter cocoa powder together before adding to the yolks. Pour in the melted and cooled butter. Using a spatula, fold in the egg whites without breaking them.

✦ Butter a round cake tin. Pour the cake mixture into the tin and bake for 30 minutes.

✦ Unmold the cake and place on a wire rack to cool at room temperature for 30 minutes.

✦ While the cake is baking, prepare the strawberry syrup. Pour all the ingredients into a saucepan. Heat over a medium heat until the sugar has dissolved completely, then reduce over a low heat for 5 minutes. Pour in the strawberry liqueur and stir. The syrup that you will use to moisten the sponge cake is now ready, set aside off the heat.

FOR THE WHIPPED CREAM
4 cups (1½ l) whipping cream
½ cup (120 g) icing sugar
1 tsp. vanilla extract

EQUIPMENT
Electric mixer
Round springform cake tin
Pastry bag
Icing turntable
Food brush
Angled spatula

✦ Now prepare the vanilla whipped cream: pour the whipping cream into the bowl, previously removed from the fridge, and mix with the icing sugar and vanilla extract. Then, using the whisk set aside in the fridge, whip the cream until stiff. Once the cream has set, pipe into a piping bag and set aside in the fridge.

✦ Now go on to assemble the cake: using a knife, carefully cut the sponge cake in half horizontally to obtain 2 discs of sponge cake. Place the first disc on a baking tray lined with plastic wrap: using a kitchen brush, soak the sponge in the strawberry syrup. Generously fill the first disc with whipped cream and place a few fresh strawberries on top. Cover with the second disc. Still using the brush, soak it in the syrup. Spread the cream over the surface of the disc to make an even, smooth layer, and smooth it with an angled spatula.

✦ Decorate with more whipped cream and serve!

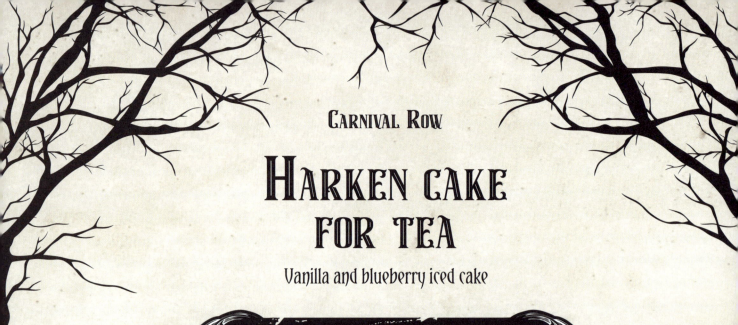

Carnival Row

Harken cake for tea

Vanilla and blueberry iced cake

> Given how... special this meeting is likely to be, you really want everything to be perfect for this moment with the Pembrokes. Afissa is really going to have to get her harken cake just right before Luisa Pembroke has anything to complain about...

LEVEL ☠
Serves 6 people
Preparation: 20 min
Cooking: 45 min

INGREDIENTS

4 eggs
⅔ cup (150 g) brown sugar
⅔ cup (160 ml) grape seed oil
1 tbsp. vanilla extract
⅔ tsp. (4 g) salt
4 tsp. (20 g) baking powder
1 cup (200 g) flour +
1 tbsp. for the candied fruit
2 tbsp. candied fruit
Butter for the tin
3 tbsp. blueberry jam

FOR THE ROYAL ICING
1 ¼ cup (300 g) icing sugar
2 egg whites, sieved
2 tbsp. (30 ml) lemon juice

EQUIPMENT
Cake mold

✦ Preheat the oven to 180°C (gas mark 4). Prepare the cake: pour the eggs into a mixing bowl and add the brown sugar, oil and vanilla extract. Whisk the mixture vigorously for 3 minutes until it is paler in color to give the mixture more volume. Set aside. Mix the salt, baking powder and flour in a bowl. Gradually add the dry ingredients to the previous mixture until smooth.

✦ Place the candied fruit in a bowl and sprinkle with flour. Mix well and remove the excess flour; set aside.

✦ Butter the cake tin and pour in the ⅔ of the cake mixture. Fold in the floured candied fruit and then evenly cover the whole with blueberry jam. Cover this layer of blueberries with the rest of the cake batter and bake for 40 to 45 minutes.

✦ Meanwhile, prepare the icing: place the icing sugar in a mixing bowl. Add the egg whites and mix until the ingredients are fully incorporated. Pour in the lemon juice and mix until smooth and glossy. Your royal icing is now ready.

✦ Remove the cake from the oven and leave to cool for 5 minutes at room temperature. Then remove from the mold and place on a wire rack. Coat with the royal icing.

DRESSING: slice this harken cake and serve it before a cup of tea!

SUPERNATURAL

METATRON'S FIRST WAFFLES

Soft waffles, chocolate coulis, vanilla whipped cream and fresh strawberries

> When you're the angel chosen by God to write his word on tablets, you know a lot about the creation of the world. And for all that, it took Metatron becoming incarnate and sitting down at table with Castiel to discover the benefits of food! Here's how to make a plate of waffles that's even more decadent and worthy of an angel!

LEVEL
Serves 4 people
Preparation: 20 min
Cooking: 30 min

INGREDIENTS

FOR WAFFLES
1 cup (250 g) sifted flour
⅔ tsp. (4 g) salt
2 tsp. (10 g) baking powder
3 whole eggs
5 tbsp. (70 g) sugar
1 ⅓ cup (300 ml) milk
1 cup (200 ml) single cream
1 ½ tbsp. (20 ml) vanilla extract
⅓ cup (80 g) melted butter
Oil or butter for the waffle iron

FOR THE MILK CHOCOLATE COULIS
1 cup (150 g) milk chocolate
⅔ cup (150 ml) single cream

FOR FINISHING
8 fresh strawberries
Maple syrup
Chantilly cream
(see tips p. 117)

EQUIPMENT
Waffle iron

✦ Mix the flour, salt and baking powder in a bowl and set aside. Break the eggs and separate the whites from the yolks. Whisk the egg whites until stiff. Pour the sugar into the yolks and whisk vigorously to whiten and increase the volume of the mixture. Pour in the milk, cream, vanilla extract and melted butter. Gradually fold the dry mixture into the liquid ingredients. Whisk until smooth. Gently fold in the egg whites.

✦ Grease and heat a waffle iron, then pour some batter into each mold. Leave to heat for 3 to 5 minutes, depending on the desired texture. You can also pour the batter into pre-greased waffle molds and bake for 15 minutes at 200°C (gas mark 6).

✦ While the waffles are cooking, prepare the chocolate coulis: crush the chocolate and place it in a double boiler. Pour the cream into a small saucepan and heat over a medium heat. Still in a bain-marie, stir the hot cream into the chocolate. Mix until you have a thick, smooth coulis. Set aside off the heat until ready to serve.

✦ Finally, prepare the fresh strawberries: rinse them under a trickle of water without removing the hulls. Dry them thoroughly with kitchen roll. Hull and cut into quarters.

DRESSING: serve the waffles piping hot. Fill the hollow compartments with chocolate coulis and maple syrup. Add a generous amount of Chantilly cream and don't forget the fresh strawberries! You can also make a salted butter caramel coulis (tips p. 115).

Buffy the Vampire Slayer

Jelly for Xander

Pomegranate and hibiscus jelly

> It's a good thing Xander was a bit peckish and loves fruit jelly, otherwise he'd never have got into the kitchen, and would never have caught the canteen maid poisoning your dessert...

LEVEL ☠
Serves 4 people
Preparation: 5 min
Cooking: 15 min
Rest: 1 h

INGREDIENTS

2 ½ cups (600 ml) water
1 ⅓ cup (300 ml) pomegranate juice
A few hibiscus leaves
2 cups (400 g) sugar
¾ tsp. (4 g) agar-agar

✦ In a saucepan, bring the water to the boil, add the pomegranate juice and dip the hibiscus leaves in. Keep at a gentle boil for 5 minutes, then remove the hibiscus and add the sugar and agar-agar.

✦ Bring to the boil and cook for 10 minutes, stirring with a whisk.

✦ Pour the mixture into a dish. Once it has reached room temperature, set the jelly aside in the fridge for at least 1 hour to allow it to set. Then you can enjoy it!

LOCKE AND KEY

The Rolls of Remembrance

Cinnamon rolls

What if you could delve into your memories and relive some of the most important moments in your life? You could feel the joy and peace of that time... Like the time you baked cinnamon rolls for your husband to tell him you were expecting your third child...

LEVEL ☠
Serves 6 people
Preparation: 15 min
Cooking: 40 min
Rest: 2 h

INGREDIENTS

FOR DOUGH
⅔ tbsp. (10 ml) whole milk
1 tbsp. (15 g) dry baker's yeast
3 organic whole eggs + 2 organic egg yolks
1 cup (200 g) cold butter
1 ¼ cup (300 g) all-purpose flour + a little to work the dough
1 tsp. (5 g) salt
2 tbsp. (30 g) soft brown sugar
2 tbsp. maple syrup
1 ½ tbsp. (20 ml) vanilla extract
Oil for the mould

FOR THE GARNISH
⅓ cup (80 g) semi-salted butter, at room temperature
4 tbsp. brown sugar
1 tbsp. ground cinnamon

FOR THE GLAZING
2 egg yolks
2 tbsp. milk

FOR THE ICING
7 tbsp. (100 ml) sweetened condensed cream

EQUIPMENT
Food processor and dough hook
Rolling pin
Food brush
Flexible spatula
Baking dish

✦ Allow the milk to come to room temperature then pour into a bowl and add the yeast. Stir and set aside for 5 minutes to activate.

✦ In another bowl, lightly beat the eggs and egg yolks. Separately, cut the butter into small cubes and chill in the fridge; the butter must be cold before it can be incorporated.

✦ Pour the flour into the bowl of a food processor fitted with a dough hook. Add the salt, sugar, maple syrup, vanilla extract, beaten eggs and activated yeast. Knead on a medium speed for 2 minutes, then faster for 5 minutes until you have an almost homogenous ball that no longer sticks to the bowl. While continuing to knead, add the butter. After 2 minutes, the dough should be smooth.

✦ Cover and set aside under a damp cloth for 1 hour.

✦ During this time, prepare the filling: place the butter in a bowl and using a flexible spatula, work it until it has the texture of buttercream. Stir in the brown sugar and ground cinnamon.

✦ When the dough has rested, place it on a floured work surface. Punch the dough to knock it back, releasing air. Flour the rolling pin and roll out the dough to a thickness of 3 mm to make a long, wide layer. Coat the dough with the cinnamon mixture. Then roll the dough into a long sausage. Cut into 4 to 5 cm pieces.

✦ Oil a large casserole dish and lay the raw cinnamon rolls flat, at least 5 cm apart. Cover with a damp cloth and leave to rise again for 1 hour.

✦ Preheat the oven to 180°C (gas mark 4). Beat the egg yolks in a bowl and stir in the milk. Brush the rolls with the beaten egg yolks and bake for 40 minutes.

DRESSING: drizzle the rolls with sweetened condensed milk while they are still warm. Leave them to cool for a few moments before eating them!

CRIMSON PEAK

THE OPERA OF DEPARTURE

Coffee and praline opera

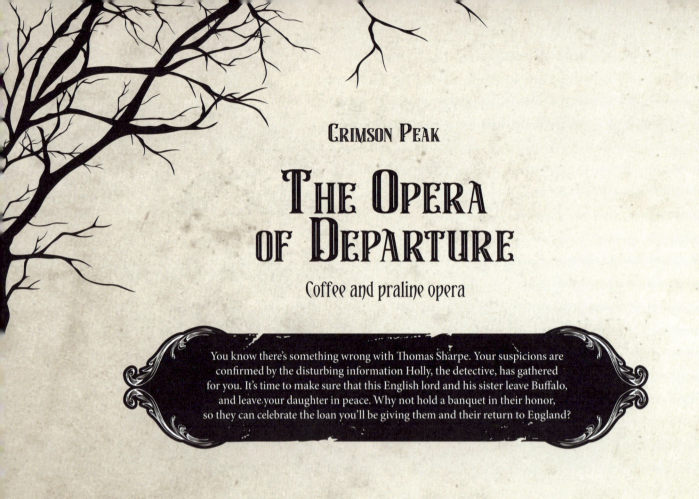

You know there's something wrong with Thomas Sharpe. Your suspicions are confirmed by the disturbing information Holly, the detective, has gathered for you. It's time to make sure that this English lord and his sister leave Buffalo, and leave your daughter in peace. Why not hold a banquet in their honor, so they can celebrate the loan you'll be giving them and their return to England?

LEVEL ☠☠
Serves 6 people
Preparation: 30 min
Cooking: 20 min
Rest: 4 h

INGREDIENTS

3 square sheets of almond sponge cake cut by 20 cm each (for the recipe see tips on p.117)

FOR THE COFFEE BUTTERCREAM
½ cup (125 g) butter at room temperature
½ cup (125 g) sugar
1 tsp (5 ml) water
4 egg yolks
2 tbsp. coffee extract
1 tbsp. coffee liqueur

FOR THE PRALINE GANACHE
⅓ cup (80 g) hazelnuts
7 tbsp. (100 g) sugar
1 cup (250 g) dark chocolate
½ cup (125 g) whipping cream
1 tsp. grapeseed oil (optional)

✦ Prepare your coffee cream: place the butter in a bowl and work it into a creamy consistency using a flexible spatula. Set aside.

✦ Pour the sugar and water into a saucepan and heat over a medium heat to melt the sugar. Cook for 8 to 10 minutes, until the syrup has passed the boiling point and reached 121°C.

✦ Pour the egg yolks into a mixing bowl. Once the syrup has reached the right temperature, add it to the egg yolks by pouring it down the side of the bowl while whisking well. The idea is to emulsify the egg yolks and give the mixture volume. Gradually fold in the softened butter. Finally, pour in the coffee extract and coffee liqueur. Cover the bowl with plastic wrap and keep it in a cool place.

✦ Prepare the praline ganache: start by dry-roasting the hazelnuts in a frying pan over a medium heat for 2 minutes. They should toast without burning. Set them aside.

✦ Pour the sugar into a saucepan and heat over a medium heat. Cook the sugar for a few minutes until it melts, becomes fluid and takes on a caramel colour. Pour over the roasted hazelnuts and leave to cool for 5 minutes.

✦ Meanwhile, bring a pan of water to the boil to prepare a bain-marie. Crush the chocolate and place in a mixing bowl with the cream. Melt the chocolate in the bain-marie and fold it into the liquid cream with a flexible spatula as it melts. Set the creamy mixture aside.

FOR THE CHOCOLATE ICING
8 tbsp. (120 g) dark chocolate couverture

FOR THE COFFEE SYRUP
7 tbsp. (100 ml) espresso
2 tbsp. (30 g) sugar

EQUIPMENT
Spatulas (angled and flexible)
Silicone pastry sheet
Mixer
Pastry bag
20 cm square mold
Food brush

✦ Your caramelized hazelnuts have now melted to form a nougatine. Crush the hazelnuts and mix vigorously in a mixer, alternating mixing and resting: mix for 20 seconds, leave to rest for 10 seconds then mix for 20 seconds and leave to rest for 10 seconds. Repeat these operations until you obtain a doughy mixture with a nutty flavor. If your mixture lacks fluidity, pour in the grapeseed oil. Once you have obtained your praline, fold it into the chocolate ganache. Pipe into a piping bag. Set aside.

✦ Melt the dark chocolate in a bain-marie. Set aside.

✦ Finally, prepare a coffee syrup: pour the espresso and sugar into a small saucepan and melt the sugar. Mix well and set aside.

✦ Assemble your opera: place 1 layer of almond sponge cake in the bottom of a 20 cm square mold. Brush the sponge cake with the coffee syrup. Cover the sponge cake with the coffee cream. Poach the praline ganache and spread thinly with an angled spatula. Cover with another layer of almond sponge cake and soak again. Cover with coffee buttercream, then with praline ganache. Finally, cover with the last layer of almond sponge cake. Soak it. Cover with the melted chocolate. Cover with plastic wrap and chill in the fridge for 4 hours.

DRESSING: Take the cake out of the tin and cut into rectangular slices to serve.

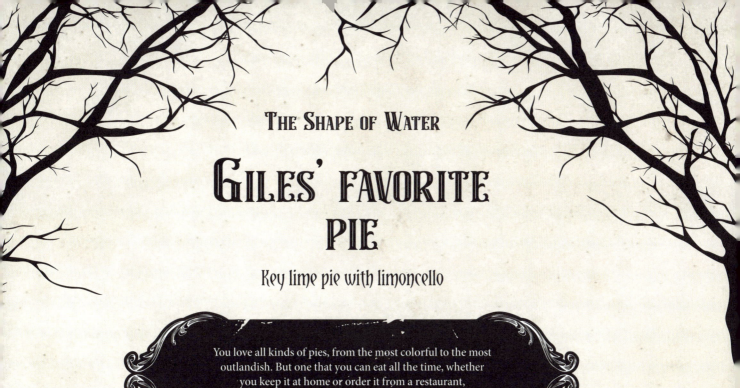

The Shape of Water

Giles' favorite pie

Key lime pie with limoncello

You love all kinds of pies, from the most colorful to the most outlandish. But one that you can eat all the time, whether you keep it at home or order it from a restaurant, is the fluorescent green key lime pie!

LEVEL ☠
Serves 6 people
Preparation: 30 min
Cooking: 25 min
Rest: 2 h

INGREDIENTS

FOR PASTE
5 tbsp. (70 g) semi-salted butter
+ a little for the tin
1 ¼ cup (300 g) tea biscuits
1 ⅓ tbsp. (20 g) flour

FOR THE LIME CREAM (THE TART SHELL)
3 cups (750 ml) sweetened condensed milk
⅔ cup (150 ml) double cream
12 untreated limes (juice and zest)
3 drops of green dye

FOR THE LIMONCELLO WHIPPED CREAM
1 cup (250 ml) whipping cream
⅔ cup (150 g) mascarpone cheese
3 ¼ tbsp. (50 g) icing sugar
1 tsp. limoncello
1 unwaxed lime

EQUIPMENT
Pie mold
Pastry bag and fluted piping nozzle

✦ Preheat the oven to 180°C (gas mark 4). Prepare the pastry: melt the butter in a bowl in the microwave or in a small saucepan. Then leave to cool.

✦ Butter a pie tin. Crush and mix the biscuits. Place them in a mold, add the flour and melted butter. Mix well. Line the cake tin with the mixture, working your way up the sides. Place in the oven for 10 minutes. Remove from the oven and set aside.

✦ Meanwhile, prepare the creamy lime custard: pour the condensed milk, cream, lime juice and zest and food coloring into a bowl. Mix well and pour into the tin with the baked biscuit base. Place in the oven for 7 minutes.

✦ Remove the pie from the oven. Leave to cool and refrigerate for at least 2 hours.

✦ Place a mixing bowl and whisk in the fridge to prepare the whipped cream.

✦ When you take the pie out of the fridge, take the chilled bowl and whisk and prepare the limoncello whipped cream: pour the liquid cream, mascarpone and sugar into a bowl. Whisk the mixture vigorously to whip the cream and gradually add the limoncello while whisking. Once the cream has set, pipe it into a piping bag fitted with a fluted tip and set aside in the fridge until ready to serve.

DRESSING: slice the lime very thinly. Take the lime pie out of the tin and pipe the limoncello whipped cream on top. Decorate with thin slices of lime before serving.

Carrie

Margaret's Apple Pie

Apple pie with spices and cider

> Your body is changing and you feel that you are no longer the young girl you were a few weeks ago. You feel that the world is angry with you, and your mother never misses an opportunity to put you down and humiliate you. Candlelit dinners with her are becoming increasingly complicated...

LEVEL ☠
Serves 6 people
Preparation: 30 min
Cooking: 35 min

INGREDIENTS

FOR PASTRY
Flour for the working space
2 cups (400 g) homemade shortcrust pastry (see tips p. 116)
1 egg yolk
3 ¾ tbsp (50 ml) milk

FOR THE APPLE FILLING
1 kg Royal Gala apples
⅓ cup (80 g) semi-salted butter + a little for the tin
1 tsp. (5 g) ground cinnamon
1 tsp. (5 g) ground nutmeg
1 tsp. (5 g) ground ginger
3 tbsp. (40 g) brown sugar
7 tbsp. (100 ml) sweet apple cider

EQUIPMENT

Rolling pin
Pie mold
Baking beans or dried beans
Food brush

✦ Preheat the oven to 200°C (gas mark 6). Flour the work surface. Divide the shortcrust pastry into 2 equal parts. Flour a rolling pin and roll out the 2 pieces into 2 discs 5 mm thick. Cut the first disc into strips. Place on a sheet of greaseproof paper and chill in the fridge. Butter and line a pie tin with the second disc. Prick the pastry base all over with the tip of a fork. Cover the pastry with baking beans to prevent it from shrinking or puffing up. Place in the oven for 12 minutes.

✦ Meanwhile, prepare the apple filling: peel the apples, remove the cores and cut into strips. Melt the butter in a large frying pan. Add the apples, spices and brown sugar. Mix well and add the sweet cider. Continue cooking over a high heat for 10 minutes, until the apples have absorbed the cider. Lower the heat and stir well to prevent the apples from sticking or burning. Set aside off the heat.

✦ Take the pie tin and fill it with the apple mixture. Cover with strips of pastry in a lattice pattern. Whisk the egg and milk together in a bowl. Using a pastry brush, brush the pastry strips with the mixture. Bake in the oven for 15 minutes.

DRESSING: You can serve this pie while still warm with a little whipped cream and vanilla ice cream.

Drinks

The Magicians

Eliot's Signature Cocktail

Vodka, mint and bitters cocktail

Eliot seems to be hiding a lot behind his casual, out-of-touch demeanor. You can tell at a glance that he's a talented sorcerer. And his gifts seem to include mixology. Why not reproduce his signature cocktail?

✦ Pour the ice cubes into a shaker, followed by the vodka and Noilly Prat®.

✦ Mix with a slotted spoon, then stir in the crème de menthe, sugar syrup and celery bitters.

✦ Mix, strain and serve immediately!

LEVEL ☠
For 1 cocktail
Preparation: 2 min

INGREDIENTS

2 large ice cubes
3 tbsp. (40 ml) vodka
1 ½ tbsp. (20 ml) Noilly Prat® vermouth
2 tbsp. (30 ml) crème de menthe
1 ½ tbsp. (20 ml) sugar syrup
4 dashes of celery bitters

EQUIPMENT

Shaker
Mixing spoon

Hocus Pocus

The Sanderson Sisters' Life Potion

Apple, cucumber and kiwi detox drink

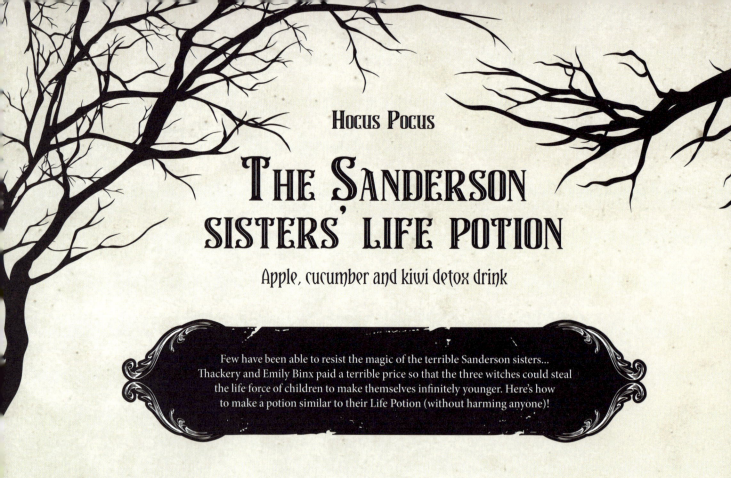

Few have been able to resist the magic of the terrible Sanderson sisters... Thackery and Emily Binx paid a terrible price so that the three witches could steal the life force of children to make themselves infinitely younger. Here's how to make a potion similar to their Life Potion (without harming anyone)!

LEVEL ☠
Serves 4 drinks
Preparation: 15 min

INGREDIENTS

2 cucumbers
2 Granny-Smith apples
3 kiwis
2 lemons (juice)
3 tbsp. (50 g) spinach shoots
2 tbsp. honey
4 large ice cubes
1 drop of green food coloring (optional)
2 tsp. green edible powder

EQUIPMENT
Mixer
Cocktail spoon
and filter

✦ Cut the cucumbers in half and remove the seeds. Do the same with the apples and kiwis. Squeeze the lemons.

✦ Place the fruit and lemon juice in the bowl of a blender with the spinach, honey and ice cubes, and blend vigorously for 30 seconds until smooth.

✦ Strain the mixture before serving chilled.

✦ If you want to give your drink even more colour, add a drop of green coloring. Finally, pour ½ tsp. green edible powder into each of the 4 glasses and stir with a cocktail spoon.

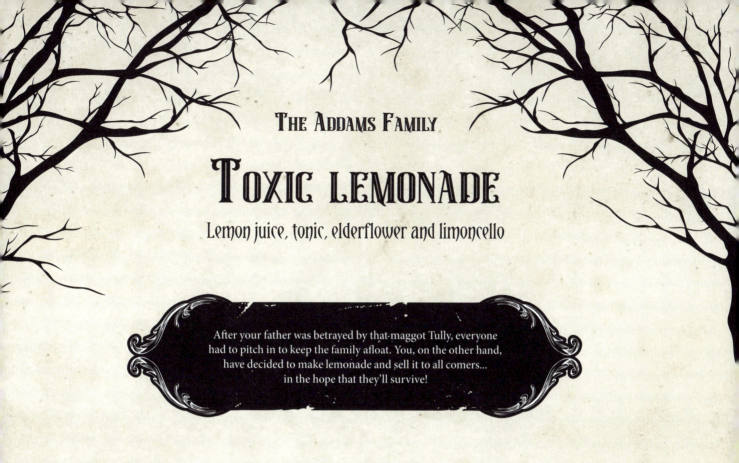

The Addams Family

Toxic Lemonade

Lemon juice, tonic, elderflower and limoncello

> After your father was betrayed by that maggot Tully, everyone had to pitch in to keep the family afloat. You, on the other hand, have decided to make lemonade and sell it to all comers… in the hope that they'll survive!

LEVEL ☠
For 1 glass
Preparation: 2 min

INGREDIENTS

½ organic lemon (juice)
1 ½ to 3 tbsp. (20 to 40 ml) limoncello
⅔ tbsp. (10 ml) elderberry syrup
2 tbsp. crushed ice or 2 large ice cubes
7 tbsp. (100 ml) sparkling water or tonic, well chilled

✦ Pour the lemon juice, limoncello and elderberry syrup into a tall glass and mix well.

✦ Add the ice and stir for a few seconds before adding the soft drink.

✦ Serve immediately!

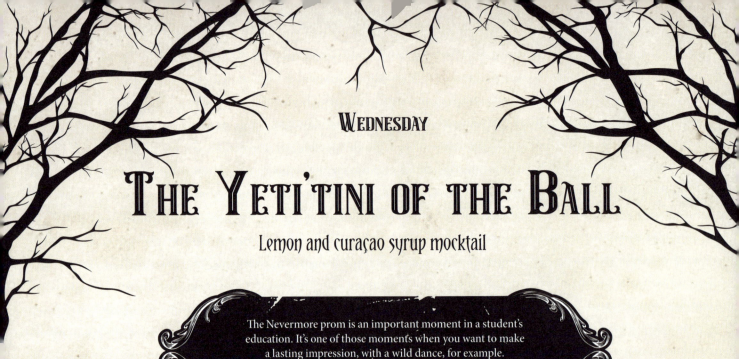

Wednesday

The Yeti'tini of the Ball

Lemon and curaçao syrup mocktail

The Nevermore prom is an important moment in a student's education. It's one of those moments when you want to make a lasting impression, with a wild dance, for example. Why not pour yourself an ice-cold mocktail before stretching your legs on the dance floor?

LEVEL ☠
For 1 cocktail
Preparation: 5 min

INGREDIENTS
1 ½ tbsp. (20 ml) blue curaçao syrup
1 ½ tbsp. (20 ml) lime juice
1 tbsp. crushed ice or
1 stick dry ice (see tips p. 121)
7 tbsp. (100 ml) tonic or lemonade

EQUIPMENT
Martini glass
Cocktail spoon

✦ Pour the curaçao, lemon juice and crushed ice into a martini glass.

✦ Mix with a cocktail spoon before adding tonic or lemonade.

✦ Enjoy immediately.

NOTE
If you use a dry ice stick, please read our short instructions for use. You should enjoy your cocktail but never swallow the dry ice stick, otherwise you could seriously injure yourself.

Ash vs Evil Dead

Ash's Pink Fu**ck!

Vodka, strawberry and citrus cocktail

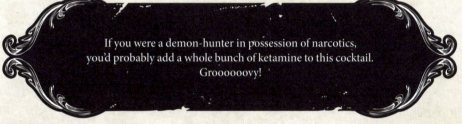

If you were a demon-hunter in possession of narcotics, you'd probably add a whole bunch of ketamine to this cocktail. Grooooooovy!

LEVEL ☠
For 1 cocktail
Preparation: 5 min

INGREDIENTS

3 tbsp. (40 ml) vodka
1 ½ tbsp. (20 ml) strawberry liqueur
1 dash grenadine syrup
5 tbsp. (80 ml) lemonade
1 organic orange (zest) + 1 orange slice
3 ice cubes

EQUIPMENT

Boston shaker
Old Fashioned glass
or whisky glass

✦ Pour the vodka, strawberry liqueur, grenadine and lemonade into a Boston shaker with the ice cubes.

✦ Stir vigorously for 15 seconds and pour into an Old Fashioned or whisky glass!

✦ Zest the orange over the glass and garnish with a slice of orange. Enjoy immediately.

Evil Dead

Bloody Party

Bloody Mary revisited

There's something mysterious and gloomy about this cabin deep in the woods.
You've come here for a weekend with friends and the place is remote.
While you're enjoying an evening of macaroni and cocktails,
you come across some strange objects, an old book... and a tape recorder...
Why not listen to what it has to say?

✦ Place all the ingredients in the bowl of a blender (except the 4cl bourbon). Blend vigorously for 30 seconds and pour into 4 tall glasses.

✦ Pour 10 ml of bourbon onto the surface of each glass using the back of a cocktail spoon. Ignite the bourbon with a blowtorch before sipping!

LEVEL ☠
Serves 4 drinks
Preparation: 5 min

INGREDIENTS

2 cups (500 ml) tomato juice
7 tbsp. (100 ml) bourbon
2 tsp. (10 ml) maple syrup
1 ½ tbsp. (20 ml) lemon juice
4 tsp. (20 ml) Tabasco® sauce
1 tsp. celery salt
4 large ice cubes

TO SERVE
3 tbps. (40 ml) bourbon

EQUIPMENT
Blender
Kitchen torch
Cocktail spoon

TIPS

The Sauces

Ketchup

FOR 1 SMALL BOTTLE - PREPARATION: 10 MIN
COOKING: 30 MIN

INGREDIENTS
1 clove of garlic
1 red onion
6 ripe tomatoes
2 tbsp. olive oil
2 pinches ground cumin
2 pinches ground ginger
2 tbsp. tomato paste
1 ½ tbsp. (20 g) brown sugar
7 tbsp. (100 ml) red wine vinegar, freshly ground pepper

EQUIPMENT
Hand blender
Conical strainer

- Prepare the vegetables: peel the garlic and onion. Chop them finely and set aside. Peel the tomatoes and cut them into large chunks. Set aside.

- Heat the olive oil in a saucepan over a medium heat. Add the garlic and onion and sauté for 3 minutes. Sprinkle with the cumin and ground ginger and stir in the tomato paste. Using a wooden spoon, mix well and add the crushed tomatoes. Mix well and add the brown sugar. Bring to the boil, then simmer over a low heat, covered, for 15 minutes, then uncovered for a further 10 minutes, until the mixture reduces. Stir in the wine vinegar and season with salt and pepper.

- Finally, using an immersion blender, blend the mixture for 2 minutes and strain through a sieve. Leave to cool before bottling.

Mayonnaise

SERVES 4 PEOPLE - PREPARATION TIME: 7 MIN

INGREDIENTS
1 extra-fresh organic egg yolk
1 tbsp. mustard
1 cup (200 ml) vegetable oil
Salt

- Prepare the mayonnaise: note that it is essential for all the ingredients to be at the same temperature for the emulsion to take place.

- Place the egg yolk and mustard in a mixing bowl. Using a whisk or fork, mix while pouring in the oil in 1 thin continuous stream. Keep mixing until the mayonnaise comes together. Add salt to taste.

- Store the mayonnaise in the fridge, closely covered to prevent crusting.

Tsuyu sauce

• Start by pouring all the ingredients into a saucepan.
• Bring to the boil.
• Strain and leave to cool before serving.

PREPARATION: 10 MIN
COOKING: 5 MIN

INGREDIENTS
5 tbsp. (80 ml) soy sauce
3 tbsp. (40 ml) mirin
2 tbsp. sugar
1 pinch grated dried bonito (katsuobushi)
7 tbsp. (100 ml) water

Salted butter caramel coulis

• Pour the cream into a small saucepan and heat over a medium heat until it comes to the boil.

• In another saucepan, pour in the sugar and water and heat until the mixture takes on a lovely amber color. Remove the pan of caramel from the heat and gradually pour over the boiling cream, stirring briskly to blend well.

• Add the butter in pieces and mix until your mixture has the consistency of a liquid, viscous coulis. Transfer to a bowl and leave to cool.

PREPARATION: 10 MIN
COOKING: 10 MIN

INGREDIENTS
7 tbsp. (100 ml) single cream
½ cup (100 g) sugar
7 tbsp. (100 ml) water
⅔ tbsp. (10 g) semi-salted butter

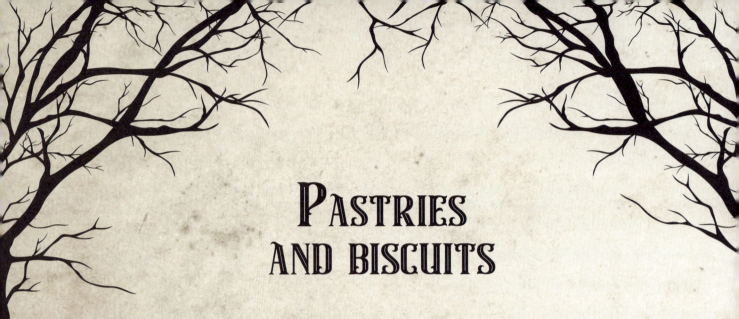

Pastries and biscuits

Shortcrust pastry

PREPARATION: 10 MIN
REST: 2 H

INGREDIENTS
2 cups (250 g) flour
1 tsp. (5 g) salt
½ cup (125 g) cold butter
½ cup (125 g) very cold water

- Place the flour and salt in a mixing bowl. Mix well and add the butter in pieces. Knead the mixture by hand for 2 minutes, then rub it between your fingers.
- Pour in the ice water all at once to create a thermal shock and knead again for 1 minute, until it forms a homogeneous ball.
- Cover with plastic wrap and refrigerate for 2 hours.
- Your shortcrust pastry is ready to use.

Pizza dough

PREPARATION : 15 MIN
REST : 1 H 30

INGREDIENTS
1 ⅓ cups (150 g) 00 or T4 flour
7 tbsp. (53 g) fresh yeast
½ tsp. (3 g) salt
⅓ cup (85 g) warm water
1 tsp. (4 g) olive oil

- Pour the flour, baking powder and salt into a mixing bowl. Mix well, distributing the fresh yeast evenly throughout the mixture.
- Add the warm water and mix quickly. Leave to stand for a few moments.
- Knead vigorously for 5 to 8 minutes. Add the olive oil and knead for a further 2 minutes.
- Place the dough in a bowl and cover with a damp cloth. Leave to rest for 1 hour.
- Knead for a further 2 minutes to remove the gas. Separate into dough pieces. Cover and leave to rest for a further 30 minutes. Roll out before adding topping.

Almond Sponge Cake

PREPARATION: 10 MIN
COOKING: 10 MIN

INGREDIENTS
1 cup (100 g) icing sugar
¾ cup (95 g) ground almonds
3 eggs
¼ cup (35 g) flour
80 g egg whites
4 ¾ tsp (15 g) caster sugar

- Preheat the oven to 180°C (gas mark 4).
- Mix the sugar and ground almonds in a bowl. In another bowl, beat the eggs and add the sugar-almond mixture until smooth. Mix until the mixture has the texture of a ribbon. Stir in the flour and set aside for a few moments to make a French meringue.
- Place the egg whites in a mixing bowl. Using an electric mixer or a whisk, beat the egg whites: once they have doubled in volume, add the sugar and continue beating until the egg whites are stiff. Gently fold them into the previous mixture using a spatula.
- Line a baking tray with baking parchment. Pour over the sponge cake mixture and bake for 10 minutes.

Creams

Lemon curd

PREPARATION TIME: 10 MIN

INGREDIENTS
4 eggs
½ cup (80 g) soft butter
Juice of 2 organic lemons
1 cup (150 g) sugar

- Crack the eggs in a saucepan with the butter, cut into pieces. Add the lemon juice and sugar to the pan. Put over a low heat and, using a whisk, stir until the butter has completely melted and the mixture has coagulated for the first time.
- Remove the pan from the heat as soon as the first bubbles appear on the surface of the cream. Strain through a cheesecloth to retain only the concentrate. Pour the lemon curd into an airtight container. You can keep it in the fridge for up to 7 days.

Chantilly cream

PREPARATION TIME: 10 MIN

INGREDIENTS
2 cups (50 cl) heavy cream
(over 30% fat)
⅓ cup (50 g) icing sugar

It's quite simple to make a Chantilly cream, you just need to know the little trick in the recipe: use very cold whipping cream and a very cold bowl and whisk.

- Place the bowl and whisk attachment (or the paddles of your electric mixer) in the freezer for a few minutes until cold. Pour in the whipping cream and icing sugar and whip vigorously until the whipped cream is stiff and forms a beak at the end of the whisk. And that's it!

The broths

Vegetable broth

FOR 1 L OF STOCK - PREPARATION: 5 MIN - COOKING: 2 H - REST: 30 MIN

INGREDIENTS
4 carrots
1 leek white
½ stalk celery
1 onion
1 bouquet garni (1 green leek, 4 sprigs of parsley, 1 sprig of fennel, 1 bay leaf, 1 sprig of parsley) of thyme)
1 shallot
8 cups (2 l) water
⅔ cup (150 ml) white wine
1 star anise
3 cardamoms

EQUIPMENT
Conical strainer

- Dice the carrots. Cut the leek, celery and onion into small pieces.
- Put all the ingredients in a casserole dish and simmer, covered, for 2 hours.
- Leave to stand for 30 minutes off the heat, then strain the stock.

Beef broth

FOR 2 L OF STOCK - PREPARATION: 20 MIN
COOKING: 4 H 15 - REST: A FEW HOURS

INGREDIENTS
1.1 lbs (500 g) beef (chuck)
Salt
1 garlic clove
2 carrots
2 onions
7 tbsp. grapeseed oil
⅓ cup (50 g) soft butter
8 cups (2 l) water
1 bouquet garni (thyme and bay leaves in a green leek leaf)
1 rosemary sprig
2 juniper berries
1 pinch cracked pepper

EQUIPMENT
Conical strainer

- Preheat the oven to 150°C (gas mark 2). Cut the meat into large cubes. Season with salt and set aside. Crush the garlic under the blade of your knife. Rinse and dry the carrots without peeling them. Quarter the onions with their skins. Pour the grapeseed oil and butter into a casserole dish and heat over a medium heat. Once the pan is hot, sauté the garlic, carrots and onions. Increase the heat and sear the meat on all sides. Once the meat is nicely colored, add the water, bouquet garni, rosemary, juniper berries and pepper. Mix well and cover.
- Bake in the oven for 4 hours.
- Once cooked, strain the contents of the casserole dish through a strainer. Leave the stock to cool before placing in the fridge.
- After a few hours, a film of fat should form. Skim it to remove the fat from your meat stock.

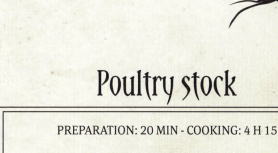

Poultry stock

PREPARATION: 20 MIN - COOKING: 4 H 15

INGREDIENTS
4 pounds (2 kg) rabbit or poultry carcass
7 tbsp. (100 ml) grapeseed oil
⅓ cup (50 g) soft butter
1 garlic clove
2 shallots
8 cups (2 l) water
1 bouquet garni (thyme and bay leaves in a green leek leaf)
1 rosemary sprig
2 juniper berries
1 pinch cracked pepper

- Preheat the oven to 150°C (gas mark 2). Crush the rabbit or poultry carcass and brown in a casserole dish with the grape seed oil and butter. Stir and simmer over a medium heat until the carcass turns a light colour. Remove from the pan.
- Skim the fat from the stewpot with a small ladle, keeping the juices at the bottom. Simmer the garlic and shallots in these juices for 5 minutes over a medium heat. Pour in the water and add the bouquet garni before placing in the oven to cook for 4 hours. 30 minutes before the end of the cooking time, add the sprig of rosemary, juniper berries and cracked pepper, and place in the oven again. This infusion will add strength and flavor to your stock.
- At the end of the 4-hour cooking time, strain the contents of the stewpot to retain only the juice and set aside.

Basic Recipes

Burger buns

PREPARATION: 15 MIN

REST: 1 H 15

COOKING TIME: 20 MIN

INGREDIENTS
1 ⅓ cups (340 g) T55 flour
1 sachet baking powder
2 tsp. (6 g) salt
2 tsp. (6 g) sugar
1 cup (200 ml) warm milk
6 tbsp. (55 g) butter cut into pieces
1 egg yolk

EQUIPMENT
Food processor
Food brush

- Place the flour, baking powder, salt and sugar in a bowl and mix well. Add the warm milk. Knead with your fingertips to obtain a smooth mixture.
- Place the mixture in the bowl of a food processor and pulse on low speed for 2 to 3 minutes. Add the butter to the bowl and pulse for a further 7 minutes, until the dough is smooth and glossy.
- Cover the dough with a tea towel and leave to develop for 45 minutes.
- Flour your work surface: place the pastry on it and remove the gas. Divide the dough into 4 equal pieces.
- Shape them by folding the dough inwards. Repeat until you obtain uniform balls. Flour them, and your hands if necessary, to make them easier to handle. Cover again and leave to rise for a further 30 minutes.
- Brush with egg yolk and bake for 20 minutes.

Red onion pickles

FOR A 1 L JAR
PREPARATION: 10 MIN
REST: 30 MIN
STORAGE: SEVERAL MONTHS IN THE REFRIGERATOR

INGREDIENTS
8 red onions
⅔ cup (100 g) sugar
1 cup (200 ml) spirit vinegar
1 ⅓ cup (300 ml) water

Here's a very simple recipe for pickles, based on the 1-2-3 rule: 1 part sugar, 2 parts vinegar, 3 parts water. You can add herbs and condiments if you feel like it.

• Start by peeling and chopping the red onions. Place in an airtight jar. Set aside.

• Pour the remaining ingredients into a saucepan and bring to the boil. Keep boiling until the sugar has dissolved. Pour the boiling mixture over the onions in the jar and close. Leave to stand for 30 minutes at room temperature.

• Open the jar, close it and place it in the fridge to store your pickles. And that's it!

Crushed ice or dry ice sticks

Dry ice is actually solidified carbon dioxide. While its use creates quite a spectacle, it's important to remember that dry ice should only be used with care, and I can't stress this enough.

Here are a few rules to follow:

• Dry ice should not be handled with bare hands, as its temperature of -78°C can cause blisters or burns. So always wear gloves and, if possible, handle the ice with ice tongs or a spoon. If you can, be sure to wear protective goggles, which are very useful in the event of splashing.

• Dry ice should be handled with care. Children are not allowed to use it. Dry ice should only be stored in special containers.

• For a glass of cocktail at room temperature, use only a 2 cm long stick. Your drink will be chilled in less than 1 minute.

• The smoke from the dry ice is not toxic, but the stick in the cocktail glass is. So don't eat what's left of the dry ice at the bottom of your glass.

Culinary and Gourmet Lexicon

A

Agar-agar
A natural gelling agent used in the preparation of fruit coulis, jams, fondants and purées.

B

Bain-marie
Also called 'double boiler', it is a cooking technique consisting of heating a container by placing it on the surface of a quantity of boiling water.

Baker's yeast
Yeast made up of micro-organisms which, by feeding on the compounds in the environment in which they are introduced, produce gases which cause the dough to grow and swell.

Baking powder
A leavening powder generally composed of edible sodium bicarbonate (acting as a basic agent), an acid and a stabilizer (such as starch). The leavening action occurs through a chemical reaction once this powder has been mixed with a moist device. These chemical reactions produce gases that increase the volume of doughs and cakes.

Baking soda
A chemical substance with many useful properties in cooking. Not to be confused with technical bicarbonate, sodium bicarbonate is used in baking to make preparations rise. It can also be used to tenderise meat when placed in a marinade. Beware of the salty taste it can bring if used in the wrong proportions.

Beat
To whisk a preparation vigorously in order to integrate all its ingredients or increase its volume.

Blanch
Whisk the eggs and sugar vigorously to obtain a frothy, pale yellow to white mixture.

C

Chop finely
To reduce a food into small pieces using a knife, chopper or food processor.

Coat
Butter or flour the sides of a mould to prevent the mixture from sticking. You can also line a mold with pastry, cream or meringue.

Compote
Cover and cook slowly over a low heat until the consistency of a compote is obtained.

Coulis
Liquid purée obtained by slow cooking.

Crush
Break or cut fruit, vegetables, dried fruit, or chocolate into irregular pieces.

D

Deglazing
This consists of dissolving and recovering the substances (cooking juices) attached to the bottom of a pan or dish using a liquid added at the end of cooking, such as water, wine, cream, etc.

Details
Cut out shaped pieces of food or pastry with a knife or cookie cutters.

F

Filling
Mixture of ingredients.

Flour
Dust a surface with flour to prevent it sticking.

G

Grapeseed oil
Grapeseed oil is fairly easy to find in the oil section of supermarkets. Rich in fatty acids, it has a high smoke point (the temperature at which oil smokes and breaks down) and can therefore be used for cooking without over-flavouring preparations.

H

Hull
Remove the skin from the almonds, hazelnuts, pistachios or tomatoes after scalding them for a few moments.

J

Julienne
Cut vegetables or herbs into small pieces or thin strips.

L

Line
Line a mold or circle with pastry to form a base that can be filled or topped.

M

Mascarpone
A rich Italian cow's milk cheese, generally used in traditional tiramisu but also in cheesecake.

Mixing bowl
Half-sphere-shaped bowl, usually made of stainless steel

P

Pastry cutter
An instrument used to cut out pieces of a given shape from a dough (a cake or a rolled-out biscuit) under the effect of impact or pressure. Cookie cutters come in a variety of shapes, from metal to thick plastic.

Poach
To cook food in a simmering liquid.

R

Reduce
To heat a preparation so that the water it contains evaporates, thickens its consistency and concentrates its flavors.

Roast
Frying a generally dry food, such as coffee beans, almonds or cloves, without fat, to release its aromas.

Rubber spatula
A flexible spatula used to scrape the sides of a container to recover as much material as possible.

S

Shape
Use your hands to shape the dough.

Sieve
Pass a powdered ingredient (flour or sugar, for example) through a sieve or chinois strainer to remove any lumps or clumps.

Slice finely
Cut foodstuff, meat or vegetables, into very thin slices that are easier to cook.

Softened butter
The consistency of worked butter, close to that of ointment.

Springform cake tin
Mold with high, smooth or fluted edges. The base can be removed. Used for a wide range of pastries such as sponge cakes and cheesecakes.

Z

Zest
The act of removing the zest from a citrus fruit using a "zester" or vegetable peeler. The zest can be used to flavor a cream or any other preparation, either by leaving it in a ribbon or by grating it.

Conversions

Spoon / weight

ELEMENT	TEASPOONS	TABLESPOONS
Powdered sugar	5 g	15 g
Flour, Semolina	4 g	12 g
Butter	5 g	15 g
Fresh cream	5 ml	15 ml
Oil	5 ml	15 ml
Salt	5 g	15 g
Pepper	2 g	5 g

Food / weight

HOW MUCH DOES...
1 knob butter	5 g
1 pinch of salt	1 g
1 egg	55 g
1 onion	60 g
1 tomato	60 g
1 potato	100 g

Volume / weight

VOLUME	WEIGHT
1 ml	1 g
1 cl	10 g
1 dl	100 g
1 l	1000 g

Oven temperatures

Gas mark 1/4	110°C	Gas mark 5	190°C
Gas mark 1/2	120°C	Gas mark 6	200°C
Gas mark 1	140°C	Gas mark 7	220°C
Gas mark 2	150°C	Gas mark 8	230°C
Gas mark 3	160°C	Gas mark 9	240°C
Gas mark 4	180°C		

Seasonal Fruit and Vegetables

	Vegetables	Fruits
Spring	Artichoke Asparagus Aubergine Beans Beetroot Carrot Cauliflower Celery Courgette Cucumber Leaf salad Leek Lentils Lettuce or romaine Onion Peas Peppers Radish Red cabbage Sorrel Spinach Sweet pea Tomato Turnip Watercress	Apple Apricot Banana Blackberry Blackcurrant Cherry Fresh almonds Melon Plum Raspberry Rhubarb Strawberry Wild strawberry
Summer	Artichoke Batavia Beans Beetroot Broccoli Brussels sprouts Carrot Cauliflower Courgette Cucumber Eggplant Fennel Garlic Gherkin Green bean Leek Lentils Lettuce Maize Mesclun Onion Peppers Radish Red cabbage Salad Salsify Sorrel Spinach Squash Swiss chard Tomato Turnip Watercress	Almond Apple Apricot Banana Blackberry Blackcurrant Blueberry Cherry Fig Grape Melon Mirabelle Nectarine Peach Pear Plum Raspberry Redcurrant Strawberry Watermelon Wild strawberry

	Vegetables	Fruits
Fall	Beetroot Bolet Broccoli Brussels sprouts Carrot Cauliflower Celery Chard Chinese leaf Endive Fennel Jerusalem artichoke Lamb's lettuce Leek Lettuce Maize Mushrooms Onion Parsnip Porcini mushroom Pumpkin Radish Salad Salsify Spinach Squash Trumpet of death Turnip Watercress	Apple Banana Blueberry Chestnut Clementine Fig Grape Kiwi Olive Orange Pear Plum Quince Tangerine Vineyard peach Walnut
Winter	Artichoke Beetroot Broccoli Brussels sprouts Cabbage Cardoon Carrot Cauliflower Celery Dandelion Endive Jerusalem Lamb's lettuce Leek Onion Parsnips Pumpkin Radish Salsify Sorrel Spinach Squash Tangerine Turnip Watercress	Advocado Apple Banana Blood orange Clementine Grapefruit Guava Kiwi Lemon Lychee Mango Orange Papaya Passion fruit Pear Persimmon Pineapple Pomegranate Pomelo

The knives

Fillet knife
15 to 22 cm knife with very fine blade, useful for filleting fish.

Chef's knife
20-30 cm thick-bladed knife for chopping, slicing and mincing. It is mainly used in cooking, and increasingly in its serrated blade form; the serrations create cushions of air which prevents food from sticking to the blade.

Paring knife
7 to 10 cm knife with thick, short blade and very sharp. It is used for peeling and removing stalks, roots etc.

The butcher's cleaver
The "feuille de boucher", also known as the "Couperet", is a knife weighing between 500 and 850 g, depending on the model and size of blade chosen, from 24 to 30 cm long. This knife will enable you to handle small and medium-sized cuts such as pork chops, rabbit, etc. Reinforced models, allow you to break thicker bones and work with large cuts, such as game.

Julienne cut

Cut the vegetables into sticks 3 to 5 cm long and 1 to 2 mm thick.

Carving in Mirepoix

Dice the vegetables into 1 to 2 cm cubes.

Blood

Fresh blood is easy to obtain from a butcher. All you have to do is ask him to reserve the quantity needed for the recipe a few days in advance.

Index of ingredients

A

Abondance cheese – 52
Agar-agar – 86
Apples
    Apple – 73
    Granny-Smith apple – 102
    Royal Gala apple – 96
Apple cider – 96
Arborio rice – 55
Avocado – 15

B

Bacon – 25, 58
Baking powder – 25, 70, 82, 85
Basil – 34
Batavia lettuce – 26
Bay leaf – 39
Beef knuckle – 119
Beef tail – 44
Beers
    Ale – 39
    Stout – 64
Beetroot – 33, 48
Biscuits
    Joconde biscuits – 90
    Tea biscuits – 95
Bluberry jam – 82
Bouquet garni – 40, 64, 118, 119
Bourbon – 26, 110
Brandy – 15
Breadcrumbs – 34

Breads
    Burger bun – 58
    Farmhouse bread – 48, 63
    Sliced bread – 26
Broccoli – 63
Broths
    Beek broth – 39, 40, 44, 64
    Chicken broth – 33, 55, 63, 64
    Vegetable broth – 16, 40, 48, 55
Brown sugar (cassonade) – 73, 89
Brown sugar (vergeoise) – 82, 89, 96
Brown mushroom – 43, 55
Butters
    Butter – 25, 34, 39, 52, 63, 64, 69, 70, 73, 74, 78, 82, 85, 89, 90, 116, 117, 119, 120
    Slightly salted butter – 89, 95, 96, 115

C

Cabbages
    Brussel sprouts – 63
    Green cabbage - 33
Carcasses
    Rabbit carcass – 119
    Chicken carcass – 119
Cardamom – 118
Carrots
    Carrot – 33, 39, 40, 43, 44, 63, 64, 118, 119
    Carrot with tops – 51
Celery – 29, 63, 118
Celery bitter – 101
Chard – 44
Cheeks
    Beef cheeks – 39

Pork cheeks – 39
Chicken – 43, 48
Chicken thighs – 33
Chilli peppers
    Calabrian pepper - 34
    Chilli pepper – 56, 58
    Espelette pepper - 15
Chives – 16
Chocolates
    Baking milk chocolate – 74, 77, 85
    Baking dark chocolate – 77
    Couverture dark chocolate – 90
Chorizo – 20, 44
Chuck steak – 63, 64, 119
Cilantro – 15, 48
Cinnamon – 25, 73, 89, 96
Cognac brandy – 15
Creams
    Crème fraîche - 95
    Crème de menthe – 101
    Liquid cream - 16, 52, 85, 90, 95, 115
    Single cream - 78, 117
    Whipped cream – 85
Cucumber – 15, 102
Cumin – 48, 63, 114

D-E

Dietary bicarbonate – 51, 58
Dried skipjack tuna (katsuobushi) – 115
Duck – 43
Egg - 15, 19, 25, 34, 39, 52, 58, 69, 70, 73, 78, 82, 85, 89, 90, 96, 114, 117, 120
Eggplant

Eggplant – 48
    Japanese Eggplant – 19
Espresso – 90
Extracts
    Almond extract – 69
    Coffee extract – 90
    Vanilla extract - 74, 78, 82, 85, 89

F-G

Five-spice powder – 51
Flank steak – 51
Flours (all types) - 19, 20, 25, 34, 39, 44, 69, 70, 74, 78, 82, 85, 89, 95, 96, 116, 117, 120
Garlic – 29, 34, 39, 40, 43, 44, 48, 51, 56, 58, 63, 64, 114, 119
Ginger - 51, 56, 64, 96, 114
Goat's cheese – 16
Grape - 56
Green artificial coloring – 77, 95, 102
Green beans – 51

H-I

Hazelnut – 90, 73, 74
Honey – 25
Ices
    Crushed ice – 105, 106
    Dry ice – 106
    Ice cubes - 16, 101, 103, 105, 109, 110

J-K

Jerusalem artichockes – 48
Juices
    Lemon juice – 82, 110,117
    Pomegranate juice – 86
    Tomato juice - 110
Juniper berry – 39, 64, 119
Ketchup – 15, 58
Kidney – 39
King prawn – 15, 19
Kiwi – 15, 102

L

Leaves
    Hibiscus leaves – 86
    Oak tree leaves – 56
Leek – 52, 118
Lemons
    Lemon – 102, 105
    Yellow lemon – 40
    Lime – 15, 95, 106
    Lemonade – 106, 109
    Lemon curd – 70
Lettuce – 26
Limoncello – 95, 105
Liqueurs
    Coffee liqueur – 90
    Strawberry liqueur – 78, 108
Lotus heart – 19

M-N

Manchego – 44
Marrowbone – 33
Mascarpone – 95
Mayonnaise – 26
Milks
    Milk – 85, 89, 96, 120
    Oat milk – 25
    Sweetened condensed milk – 77, 89, 95
Minced beef – 58
Mint – 16
Mirin – 115
Miso – 58
Mozzarella – 19, 20, 29
Mustard – 15, 114
'Nduja – 29
Noily Prat® – 101

Noodles – 51
Nuts
    Macadamia nut – 74
    Nutmeg – 73, 96

O

Oat – 25
Oils
    Oil – 85, 89
    Olive oil - 15, 16, 26, 29, 34, 40, 44, 48, 52, 55, 56, 114, 116
    Colza oil – 19
    Grapeseed oil - 19, 25, 33, 34, 40, 44, 51, 55, 58, 64, 82, 90, 119
    Sunflower oil - 25, 33, 34, 90, 63, 64
    Vegetable oil – 15, 39, 114
Onions
    Onion - 29, 33, 34, 40, 44, 51, 52, 55, 58, 118, 119
    Pearl onion – 64
    Red onion – 114, 121
    Spring onion – 26, 56
Orange – 109
Oregano – 20, 29

P-R

Paprika – 48, 63
Parmesan cheese – 29, 34, 55
Parsley – 15, 33, 48, 58
Pastries
    Pizza dough – 20, 29
    Shortcrust pastry – 39, 52, 73, 96
Peas – 16, 34, 55
Pecorino romano – 55
Pepperoni – 19, 20
Peppers
    Pepper - 16, 34, 40, 44, 48, 52, 55, 64, 114, 119
    Sichuan pepper – 50
Pork filet mignon – 51
Potatoes
    Baby potato – 40, 43, 63
    Potato – 16, 48, 64
    Purée potato – 44
Powders
    Bitter cacao powder – 78
    Ground almonds – 69, 117
    Ground hazelnuts - 70
Provolone – 29
Pumpkin – 73
Purées

Chilli pepper purée – 15
Hazelnut purée – 77
Raclette cheese – 20
Reblochon cheese – 20
Red onion pickles – 26
Rib steak – 58
Rosemary - 20, 39, 40, 43, 56, 119

Red pepper – 26, 34
Syrups
Blue Curaçao – 106
Elder syrup – 105
Grenadine syrup - 109
Marple syrup - 26, 63, 73, 74, 85, 89, 110
Sugar syrup – 101

S

Salami picante – 29
Salts
Celery salt – 110
Guérande salt – 43
Salt - 15, 19, 20, 25, 26, 29, 33, 34, 39, 40, 44, 48, 50, 52, 55, 56, 58, 63, 64, 70, 74, 78, 82, 85, 89, 114, 116, 119, 120
Sardine – 26
Savory – 48
Sauces
Cholula® sauce – 25
Soy sauce – 51, 115
Sriracha – 25
Tsuyu sauce – 19
Tomato sauce – 15
Shallot - 16, 39, 40, 118, 119
Shiso – 19
Smoked lard – 64
Star anise – 118
Sugars
Brown sugar – 73, 114
Icing sugar – 78, 82, 95, 117
Sugar - 26, 29, 69, 70, 73, 74, 78, 85, 86, 90, 115, 117, 120, 121
Vanilla sugar – 25
Spareribs roast pork – 40
Sparkling water – 105
Spinach – 52, 64
Sprouts
Bamboo sprout – 51
Spinach sprout – 102
Strawberry – 78, 85
Sucrine salad – 58
Sweet peppers
Sweet pepper – 48

T

Tabasco® - 110
Tagliatelle – 34
Taleggio – 20
Thyme - 20, 34, 39, 40, 43, 56
Tomatoes
Canned tomato – 20, 29
Dried tomato – 55
Tomato – 34, 56, 114
Tomato purée - 15, 33, 34, 44, 114
Tonic – 105, 106
Trout – 56
Turkey – 63

V-W

Veal escalope – 34
Vinegars
White vinegar – 121
Red vinegar – 33, 114
Vodka – 33, 101, 109
Wines
White wine – 40, 55, 118
Red wine – 44
Shaoxing wine – 51
Whisky – 15, 39

Y-Z

Yeast – 89, 116, 120
Zucchini – 19, 55

Thanks

You've now reached the end of your reading and I hope you've enjoyed it!

I traditionally begin my thanks with my dearest Bérengère; without you none of this could have happened. I say it often, and it's important. No book, no culinary adventure to the frontiers of imaginary cultures. For more than ten years, we've been sailing together and sharing everything, and for that, thank you. I can't wait for that time of the year when the house is decorated with pumpkins, candles and autumn leaves, when we can watch *Sleepy Hollow* again, warm under a blanket.

I discovered fantasy films when I was very young, but that won't be the case for you, my little Henri... With your mother, we're likely to be paying close attention. But I can't wait to share your first horror movies and magic with you. I love you, my son.

Thank you to my parents and my sister for their unwavering support, their love and their trust. I write this sentence every time because it's the most direct way of saying thank you, thank you for everything, always.

Thank you to Medhiya and Nicolas, the photography and styling team, without whom my books could not be so beautiful. Thank you for your passion and the commitment you bring to each of my books.

Thank you to my team, Baptiste, Isabelle, Maurane, Benoit and Arthur. You're a pleasure to work with.

Thank you to all the people who helped me to produce this book, with their advice, their loans and their time.

Thank you to Catherine, Timothée, Anne and Anaïs from Hachette Heroes, and I look forward to embarking on a new adventure with you! I'd also like to thank the rest of the team at the publishing house, who will bring this book to you and give it the light it deserves.

A final big thank you to my community, readers, viewers, fans of the first hour or spectators behind the scenes. Thank you. Thank you. Thank you. THANK YOU.

Butter is happiness,

Thibaud Villanova
Gastronogeek

Copyrights

The Addams Family is an Orion Pictures, Scott Rudin Productions and Paramount Pictures film, directed by Barry Sonnenfeld, based on the original work by Charles Addams.

Dracula is a character created by Bram Stoker, for which we thank him.

Beetlejuice is a film The Geffen Company and Warner Bros Pictures, directed by Tim Burton.

Batman ™ is a registered trademark of DC Comics.

Hellboy ™ is a registered trademark of Dark Horse Comics and Mike Mignola.

Buffy the Vampire Slayer is a series created by Joss Whedon, produced by Mutant Enemy and 20th Century Fox television.

Dr Strange is a registered trademark characters of Marvel Characters inc.

Fullmetal Alchemist: Brotherhood is an anime series adapted from the manga by Hiromu Arakawa.

Demon Slayer (Kimetsu No Yaiba) is a trademark of Kabushiki Kaisha Shueisha.

Charmed is a series created by Constance M.Burge and produced by Spelling Television, Northshore Productions, Paramount Pictures and Viacom Productions.

Supernatural is a series created by Eric Kripke, produced by Kripke Enterprises, Warner Bros. television, Wonderland Sound and Vision, Supernatural Film.

Witches is a film by Nicolas Roeg, based on *The Witches* by Roald Dahl, produced by Lorimar Film Entertainment and Jim Henson Productions.

Sweeney Todd: The Demon Barber of Fleet Street is a film by Tim Burton, based on the play *Sweeney Todd* by Christopher Bond, produced by DreamWorks Pictures, Paramount Pictures, Parkes/MacDonald Productions, The Zanuck Company and Image Nation.

Edward Scissorhands is a film by Tim Burton, produced by 20th Century Fox.

Pan's Labyrinth is a film by Guillermo del Toro, produced by Estudios Picasso, Tequila Gang, Esperanto Filmoj.

Evil Dead is a trademark of Renaissance Pictures Ltd.

Luigi's Mansion is a trademark of Nintendo of America.

Castlevania is a trademark of Konami Digital Entertainment Co, Ltd.

Sabrina the Teenage Witch is a trademark of Archie Comic Publications.

Wednesday is a trademark owned by Tee and Charles Addams Foundation.

Casper the Friendly Ghost is a trademark of CLASSIC MEDIA, LLC.

Crimson Peak is a film by Tim Burton, produced by Legendary Pictures.

Carrie is a film by Brian de Palma, produced by Redbank Films and Metro-Goldwyn-Mayer.

The Lost Boys is a film by Joël Schumacher, produced by Warner Bros.

It is a film by Andrés Muschietti, produced by Vertigo Entertainment, Lin Pictures, KatzSmith Productions, New Line Cinema and RatPac-Dune Entertainment, based on the novel by Stephen King.

The Magicians is a TV series broadcast on SyFy, based on the novel by Lev Grossman.

Miss Peregrine's Home for Peculiar Children is a film by Tim Burton, produced by Chemin Entertainment and Tim Burton Productions.

Hocus Pocus is a registered trademark of Disney Enterprises, Inc.

Penny Dreadful is a television series created by John Logan, originally broadcast on Showtime and produced by Desert Wolf Productions and Neal Street Productions.

Sleepy Hollow is a film by Tim Burton, produced by Mandalay Pictures and American Zoetrope.

Dark Shadows is a film by Tim Burton, based on the series by Dan Curtis, and produced by Tim Burton Productions, Village Roadshow Pictures, Warner Bros and The Zanuck Company.

Carnival Row is a television series produced by Legendary Television and Amazon Studios.

The Shape of Water is directed by Guillermo del Toro and produced by Bull Productions, TSG Entertainment and Double Dare You Productions.

Bride of Frankenstein is a film by James Whale, produced by Universal Pictures.

The Sandman is a Netflix series adapted from the work of the brilliant Neil Gaiman.

Locke and Key is a television series created by Joe Hill, produced by Genre Arts, Hard A Productions, Circle of Confusion and IDW Entertainment, based on the comic books of the same name by Joe Hill and Gabriel Rodriguez.

All rights of translation, adaptation and reproduction, total partial, for any use, by any means, are reserved for all countries. For the publisher, the principle is to use paper made of natural, renewable, recyclable fibers and manufactured from wood from forests that adopt a sustainable management system. In addition, the publisher expects its paper suppliers to sign up to a recognized environmental certification process. No part of this publication may be reproduced, stored in a retrieval system, or transmitted, in any form or by any means without the prior written permission of the publisher, nor be otherwise circulated in any form of binding or cover other than that in which it is published and without a similar condition being imposed on the subsequent purchaser.

Printed in China by LPP

Published by Titan Books, London, in 2024.

TITAN
BOOKS
A division of Titan Publishing Group Ltd
144 Southwark Street
London SE1 0UP
www.titanbooks.com

Find us on Facebook: www.facebook.com/titanbooks
Follow us on X: @TitanBooks

A CIP catalogue record for this title is available from the British Library.

© 2023, Hachette Livre (Hachette Pratique). 58, rue Jean Bleuzen - 92178 Vanves Cedex - France
MANAGEMENT: Catherine Saunier-Talec
PROJECT MANAGER: Timothée Le Mière
PROJECT MANAGERS: Anne Vallet and Anaïs Guichard, assisted by Lea Como
ARTISTIC DIRECTORS: Bérengère Demoncy
COVER DESIGN: Mélissande Mestas
DESIGN: Les PAOistes
Reviewed by Charlotte Müller
PRODUCTION: Anne-Laure Soyez
ILLUSTRATIONS: Adobestock (Cattallina, 4zevar, Louis Renaud), iStock

ISBN 9781835410967
10 9 8 7 6 5 4 3 2 1

No part of this publication may be reproduced, stored in a retrieval system, or transmitted, in any form or by any means without the prior written permission of the publisher, nor be otherwise circulated in any form of binding or cover other than that in which it is published and without a similar condition being imposed on the subsequent purchaser.